Your
Horoscope
2022

....

Sagittarius

23 November – 21 December

igloobooks

igloobooks

Published in 2021
First published in the UK by Igloo Books Ltd
An imprint of Igloo Books Ltd
Cottage Farm, NN6 0BJ, UK
Owned by Bonnier Books
Sveavägen 56, Stockholm, Sweden
www.igloobooks.com

Copyright © 2021 Igloo Books Ltd

0721 001
2 4 6 8 10 9 7 5 3 1
ISBN 978-1-80022-527-5

Written by Belinda Campbell and Denise Evans

Designed by Simon Parker
Edited by Suzanne Fossey

Printed and manufactured in China

CONTENTS

. . . .

INTRODUCTION
. . . .

This 15-month guide has been designed and written to give
a concise and accessible insight into both the nature of your
star sign and the year ahead. Divided into two main sections,
the first section of this guide will give you an overview of your
character in order to help you understand how you think,
perceive the world and interact with others and – perhaps just
as importantly – why. You'll soon see that your zodiac sign
is not just affected by a few stars in the sky, but by planets,
elements, and a whole host of other factors, too.

The second section of this guide is made up of daily forecasts.
Use these to increase your awareness of what might appear on
your horizon so that you're better equipped to deal with the
days ahead. While this should never be used to dictate your
life, it can be useful to see how your energies might be affected
or influenced, which in turn can help you prepare for what life
might throw your way.

By the end of these 15 months, these two sections should
have given you a deeper understanding and awareness of
yourself and, in turn, the world around you. There are never
any definite certainties, but with an open mind you will find
guidance for what might be, and learn to take more control
of your own destiny.

THE CHARACTER OF THE ARCHER

. . . .

A sign that loves to wonder and wander, Sagittarians are the explorers of the zodiac, both in their minds and around the globe. Born in the ninth house of the zodiac calendar that signifies growth, progress for the sake of progress is not what this sign stands for, as the journey itself will be important to this meaningful traveller, not just the destination. The Sagittarian's quest for adventure, be it intellectual or physical, can be unquenchable because their element, fire, needs constantly fuelling to keep its flames burning bright. This sign can certainly shine brighter than most, ruled by the largest and third brightest planet in the sky. Named after the Roman ruler of gods, Jupiter makes sure that Sagittarians live with confidence and luck on their side; or perhaps it's not luck, but the hand of a higher being, as this sign can be highly spiritual or religious. Whether it's the good fortune of wealth, happiness, family, or faith this sunny sign will find something in their life that makes them feel lucky to be alive.

Born at the end of autumn, Sagittarians are mutable and are perhaps the most open-minded to change of all the signs. Openness can breed honesty, which is perhaps why Sagittarians are commonly known as the zodiac's truth-tellers. Honesty is this sign's best policy, but their blunt delivery can sometimes need finessing. The Centaur Archer that symbolises Sagittarius can be an indicator of this sign's daring attitude and physical strength. With a positive energy that embraces physical challenges, Sagittarians can make fearless sports figures, like Eddie the Eagle with his record-breaking ski stunts. Above all, this sign can be an icon of inspiration, from Britney Spears to Winston Churchill, and at their core Sagittarians can motivate, bring joy, and encourage positive change.

THE CENTAUR ARCHER

Mind of a man and body of a beast, the mythological symbol of the Centaur is one of the dual signs in the zodiac. As with any dual sign, like Gemini's twins and Pisces' two fishes, there are usually two sides to them. With Sagittarians it is usually divided as their Centaur symbol suggests, by the mind and body. This sign is full of influential thinkers from William Blake to daring athletic personalities like Bruce Lee (who was also a known philosopher). The Archer signifies many of a Sagittarian's qualities: strong, daring, but perhaps none more so than this optimistic sign's ability to always look to the future. Sagittarians' aim can strike true first time, with the luck of the ruling planet Jupiter, or can dramatically miss. But fail or succeed, this hopeful sign is the embodiment of not giving up. The Archer can be dangerous, so risk-taking is usually common for many Sagittarians. As with any wild animal, the Centaur can at times feel restless, especially if they feel caged in any way. Sagittarians need to roam freely both in the mind and body to achieve their fullest potential.

JUPITER

Ruled by the largest planet in the sky, Sagittarians are hard to miss. They are watched over by Jupiter, the ruler of the gods in Roman mythology, who ruled over the sky and was usually depicted holding his trident of lightening. For most Sagittarians, the sky's the limit and they will live their lives with optimism and the desire to broaden their horizons. The sky is an important symbol in many religions and soul-searching Sagittarians may have a strong spiritual or religious faith. Jupiter is the fastest spinning planet in the solar system, resulting in it having the shortest days of all the planets, which perhaps explains Sagittarians' restlessness and desire to live each minute to its fullest. Jupiter is well known for having a red spot, which we now know to be a continuously raging storm. Whilst Sagittarians don't often lose their temper, this red spot on their ruling planet could be an indicator that when this sign is angry, it will be visible for everyone to see. Jupiter is associated with good luck, and with a daring fire sign like Sagittarius, fortune is likely to favour this brave sign.

ELEMENTS, MODES AND POLARITIES

Each sign is made up of a unique combination of three defining groups: elements, modes and polarities. Each of these defining parts can manifest themselves in good and bad ways and none should be seen to be a positive or a negative – including the polarities! Just like a jigsaw puzzle, piecing these groups together can help illuminate why each sign has certain characteristics and help us to find a balance.

ELEMENTS

Fire: Dynamic and adventurous, signs with fire in them can be extroverted. Others are naturally drawn to them because of the positive light they give off, as well as their high levels of energy and confidence.

Earth: Signs with the earth element are steady and driven with their ambitions. They make for a solid friend, parent or partner due to their grounded influence and nurturing nature.

Air: The invisible element that influences each of the other elements significantly, air signs will provide much-needed perspective to others with their fair thinking, verbal skills and key ideas.

Water: Warm in the shallows and sometimes freezing as ice, this mysterious element is essential to the growth of everything around it, through its emotional depth and empathy.

MODES

Cardinal: Pioneers of the calendar, cardinal signs jump-start each season and are the energetic go-getters.

Fixed: Marking the middle of the calendar, fixed signs firmly denote and value steadiness and reliability.

Mutable: As the seasons end, the mutable signs adapt and give themselves over gladly to the promise of change.

POLARITIES

Positive: Typically extroverted, positive signs take physical action and embrace outside stimulus in their life.

Negative: Usually introverted, negative signs value emotional development and experiencing life from the inside out.

SAGITTARIANS IN BRIEF

The table below shows the key attributes of Sagittarians.
Use it for quick reference and to understand more about this fascinating sign.

SYMBOL	RULING PLANET	MODE	ELEMENT	HOUSE
The Centaur Archer	Jupiter	Mutable	Fire	Ninth

COLOUR	BODY PARTS	POLARITY	GENDER	POLAR SIGN
Purple	Hips, Thighs, Liver	Positive	Masculine	Gemini

10

ROMANTIC RELATIONSHIPS

. . . .

Like a moth to the flame, this fire sign draws lovers into its inviting light purely by being its dynamic and sociable Sagittarian self. Confident Sagittarians are not shy of taking the lead and braving it alone, but if they can find a partner to take on their endless journeys then they can experience their greatest adventures yet. A relationship that does not compromise their individuality in any way will be essential: a Sagittarian will not happily sacrifice their own dreams for others, like, for example, Pisceans often do. They will also abhor any signs of possessiveness from their partner, so Scorpio or Taurus lovers could be problematic. Sagittarians may have trouble committing to the one partner if they feel that the relationship is binding their freedom in any way. Learning to share their time and the art of compromising will be two tricky areas in love that this sign may need to work harder at.

With free-roaming Sagittarians, the grass can have a habit of always looking greener and they may be inclined to eagerly wander from one relationship to another. If they want to find a long-lasting love that keeps the passions of their fire element burning night after night, then finding a like-minded intellectual or outdoorsy explorer to share their life with will be key. Air signs will not only keep this fire sign burning, they are also associated with the mind and ideas so could make ideal partners for a Sagittarian looking for mental stimulation from their partner. A stimulating spouse is a must, as is finding common interests, which for this positive sign may mean adventures in the great outdoors like holidays spent wild camping and roasting marshmallows on a campfire. A sign that has a matching positive energy will have a good chance of keeping up physically with this wild Centaur. Fundamentally, this forward-thinking Archer could benefit most from an open-minded partner with whom they can see a future.

ARIES: COMPATIBILITY 5/5

If Aries gets struck by one of Sagittarius' arrows it will be a sure sign of Cupid's work. This couple's compatibility is high due to their matching positivity and lively personalities. Aries may have finally found their true match in risk-taking Sagittarius. With a shared love of travel, there's unlikely to be any Sagittarius adventure that the Aries would pass up on. These two are go-getters and if they can find shared interests then this partnership is an ideal match of two pioneering signs, the Ram and Centaur happily galloping side by side.

TAURUS: COMPATIBILITY 2/5

Sagittarius is ruled by the planet Jupiter which is associated with luck, something that a Taurus doesn't always believe in, valuing hard work more. Whilst a Sagittarian values new experiences, Taureans can prefer the comforts of what they know. The biggest struggle that this fire and earth couple may have is Sagittarius' need for freedom and Taurus' tendency towards possessiveness with their partners. A claustrophobic atmosphere should be avoided, and freedom generously given in this relationship. Learn from each other, admire the faster gallop of the Centaur and equally appreciate the steady plod of the Bull.

GEMINI: COMPATIBILITY 5/5

'I love you just the way you are,' could be the vows of strongly independent signs Sagittarius and Gemini. Despite being both mutable signs that are open to adapt, there is unlikely to be anything about this match that either partner will want to change about the other. Being opposite signs on the zodiac calendar, the bond between Sagittarius and Gemini is usually going to be unique. For a sign that can become easily bored like Gemini, the adventurous Sagittarian is a perfect fit and will ensure this couple have endless days of love and fun ahead of them.

CANCER: COMPATIBILITY 1/5

The homebody Cancer might end up feeling lost with the adventuring wanderer that is Sagittarius. Daring Sagittarians can help bring out a worldlier side to Cancerians and teach them that their sense of community can stretch larger than the end of their road. With Cancer, the roaming Sagittarius can learn the benefits of settling down in a loving relationship. These two have contrasting masculine and feminine energies that can complement each other greatly if their differences are nurtured rather than discouraged. Give each other plenty of room to be and reap the rewards from when opposites attract.

LEO: COMPATIBILITY 4/5

With two fire signs like adventurous Sagittarius and spontaneous Leo, theirs is a love that will surely spark with excitement. Here is a couple that should keep their passports to hand as either one is likely to plan a surprise romantic getaway for the other with little or no notice. Leo and Sagittarius match each other with their positive energies and are probably the dynamic couple that is at the top of every party invite list. The philosophical Sagittarius and purpose-led Leo can share a powerful bond whose influence could be felt well beyond them.

VIRGO: COMPATIBILITY 2/5

Whilst the outdoorsy Sagittarius and earth sign Virgo both have a strong love for being outside in nature, they have some serious core differences, such as Virgo's love for routine and Sagittarians' dislike of the same; so these two lovers may have their work cut out for them. The wild Centaur can sometimes feel too reckless for the over-thinking Virgo as they bolt heart-first after their goals, whilst a Sagittarian might feel that the Virgoan's overactive mind is slowing them down. Find some common ground, and this mutable pair could experience an honest and thought-provoking relationship.

LIBRA: COMPATIBILITY 4/5

The good fortune of Sagittarius' Jupiter and the love of Libra's Venus could make these two lucky in love together. Fire sign Sagittarius and air sign Libra are sure to get each other hot under the collar with their complimentary elements helping to keep their passions burning. Both high energy positive signs, they should have no problem keeping up with each other's packed social schedules and will share plenty of adventures. The tactful Libra and sometimes blunt Sagittarius could clash if their ideas of commitment don't match, but they have a good chance of working out their differences and happily moving forward together.

SCORPIO: COMPATIBILITY 2/5

Sagittarius and Scorpio can have a daring partnership: whether their gamble on each other pays off is another thing entirely. The adventurous Sagittarian will help expand Scorpio's horizons and appeal to their brave side, whilst Scorpio's fixed attitude can teach the flaky Sagittarian to stay motivated and see things through. The love of Scorpio can be all encompassing and the worst thing for a Sagittarian is for them to feel like their partner is at all possessive. This is definitely not a boring love, but flexibility and growth are both key for these two getting the most out of the relationship.

SAGITTARIUS: COMPATIBILITY 4/5

An honest and awe-inspiring couple, these two lively Sagittarian intellects can have a fiery love. If any couple stood a chance with making a long-distance relationship work, it would be these two independent spirits. Two Sagittarian lovers will understand the importance of each other's independence so will be accustomed to giving each other as much breathing space as necessary. Their mutable natures make them flexible and ready for big changes in the relationship, whether it's moving to another country or starting a family. This is a pair that can inspire, spark, and dare one another to reach the highest of heights.

CAPRICORN: COMPATIBILITY 2/5

A materialist Capricorn and dazzling Sagittarius can both be guilty of feeling a little superior, which won't do in a partnership, especially when these two can have different approaches to life. The rational Capricorn may be fearful of going to daring heights with their lively Sagittarius partner but if they are open to Sagittarius' optimism, they could learn to love more bravely. Sagittarius may feel constrained by Capricorn's constant reminder that actions have consequences, but looking before they leap could be a vital lesson for a Capricorn to teach their Sagittarian partner. The key to their happiness will be embracing each other's opposites.

AQUARIUS: COMPATIBILITY 4/5

Placed two apart on the zodiac calendar, the positive energies of an Aquarian and Sagittarian can be a complementary and exciting love match. The thrilling ideas of a Sagittarius combined with the Aquarian's independent thinking can mean that these stimulating spouses will have plenty to talk about. The fire in Sagittarius brings an enthusiastic energy to the relationship and the fixed mode of Aquarius can help provide a focus to their ideas and bring them to fruition. Communal-minded Aquarius and sociable Sagittarius will likely be at the heart of their shared communities and bring great meaning to each other's lives.

PISCES: COMPATIBILITY 3/5

The roaming Sagittarius and the escapist Pisces could end up blissfully running off into the sunset together if they can learn from each other's differences. Both ruled by Jupiter, these two may indeed have been lucky to find one another. Jupiter gives Sagittarians and Pisceans a zest for life and their shared mutable modes will make their relationship open to continuous growth and change. Pisceans can lack the active side that many fire signs have, whilst Sagittarians can lack compassion which could lead to clashes with this sensitive water sign. Focus on common interests and this deep pair could go far.

FAMILY AND FRIENDS

. . . .

Friends and family of a Sagittarian should be ready to get taken on a journey. Whether it's road-tripping down Route 66 or escaping to a meditation retreat, a Sagittarian can inspire both physical journeys and mental ones, as their duality of the Centaur (half-man, half-horse) suggests. Yoga mat at the ready, water sign and spiritual Piscean friends or family members can make the perfect partner to go in search of higher meaning and mindful enlightenment with. For more physical adventures, the active fire sign of Aries will rise to a sporty Sagittarian's challenge and race them to the top of any mountain. It's not all about the thrill of life that urges this sign on in their constant state of exploration: Sagittarians enjoy finding meaning in the world and what they do. As the charitable Sagittarian races over the marathon finishing line in their banana costume, their philanthropic Cancerian friends and family members are sure to be there cheering and offering their generous support.

A Sagittarian is a known truth-teller and sometimes their candid words of advice can be felt deeply by their sensitive family and friends. Whilst honesty is an admirable quality, the way in which Sagittarians deliver their wise words to their loved ones may need some work. Scorpio is a daring friend that may be close to a Sagittarian, and whilst the Scorpion is made of hardy stuff, any water sign has a sensitive soul that the blunt words of a Sagittarian should be wary of damaging if they want to hold on to their friendships. Expert communicator Gemini and diplomatic Libra may be able to help their Sagittarian friend word things in a more tactful way so that their words inspire rather than injure.

The famous writer and Sagittarius Dale Carnegie, who wrote *How to Win Friends and Influence People*, shows just how influential the voice of a Sagittarian can be when delivered in a positive way.

Should the studious Sagittarius wish to start their own family, their love for learning will no doubt be something that they will want to pass on to their children. Sagittarians can make wonderful teachers, whether it's teaching their child to throw a ball or learn a new language; for the travelling Sagittarian, they may decide to bring their children up in a foreign country to truly broaden their horizons and give them their first taste of adventure. The Archer looks to the future, and as a parent the future of their children could be of utmost importance to this sign; planning which schools they will attend, enrolling them in sports clubs, teaching them piano may all be things that the forward-thinking Sagittarian partner thinks about early on as they encourage their child to explore their full potential. As their children grow up, and even when they become adults, the Sagittarius parent will continue to try and challenge their children and impart their wisdom.

MONEY AND CAREERS

· · · · · · · · · · · · · · · · ·

Being a certain star sign will not dictate the type of career that you have, although the characteristics that fall under each sign could help you identify the areas in which you could potentially thrive. Conversely, to succeed in the workplace, it's just as important to understand what you are good at as it is to know what you are less brilliant at so that you can see the areas in which you will need to perhaps work harder to achieve your career and financial goals.

Sagittarians understand the preciousness of time, remember Jupiter has the shortest days of all the planets, so they might not work well with colleagues prone to dithering. As a boss, Sagittarians can be inspiring, but they can also be preachy, impatient and downright mean in their critique. Sagittarians should try to appreciate that not everyone works at the same fast pace as them (Virgos especially like taking their time over projects) and what feels obvious to them sometimes needs to be pointed out to others. Sagittarians can continue to inspire by showing compassion and patience and always offering to help those that need help.

Clear career paths such as studying law, going to film-making school, or practising to become a singer could suit the Archer who has a clear aim in life. Caged within the confines of an office might not suit all Sagittarians, so finding a career that has travel prospects could appeal to this wild traveller. This highly sociable sign may enjoy a career that allows them to speak to the masses, whether it's as an academic lecturer that uses their intellect or a spiritual or religious leader that brings meaning to life. The most influential Sagittarians in their professional field, such as Steven Spielberg, Jimi Hendrix or Taylor Swift, are well loved because they have followed their dreams and help to inspire others to do the same.

The thrill-seeking Sagittarian may need to keep their wild spending in check and always use their heads when looking to invest or gamble their money, especially if they don't have endless funds to play with. Sagittarians may be interested in more high-risk investments but, being born in the ninth house of progression, they are also a fan of seeing things grow so a more secure financial venture could bring equal satisfaction as they are more likely to see their money grow steadily but surely. If lucky Jupiter is shining down on them, Sagittarians may find themselves galloping to the races with an uncanny ability to pick out the strongest horses thanks to their inner Centaur.

HEALTH AND WELLBEING

Whilst Sagittarians don't often lose their temper, the red tempestuous spot that storms constantly on their ruling planet of Jupiter can be an indicator of the public outbursts that this sign can be capable of. The positivity of Sagittarians is a noble quality, however, this dual sign has ups and downs just like the rest of the world and cannot be expected to be all smiles. Learning how to release any upset in a positive way, whether it be through attending therapy, writing poetry, or trying out a boxercise class, is important for any sign and something that Sagittarians should not neglect.

For anyone that is prone to taking risks, they understand that danger is an inevitable part of the thrill. For Sagittarians, their physical activities may include hazardous sports like mountaineering or even being a stunt double. If risk is part of a Sagittarian's daily job or an aspect of their hobby, this sign may need to take extra care of their physical and mental health so that their body and mind can endure the extra stresses put upon it. Practising yoga and meditation could be helpful exercises for bringing strength and calmness to their action-packed life. If a Sagittarian is too restless for yoga, channelling the Archer in them could be a perfect way of satisfying their need for danger in the safety of a controlled environment of an archery class.

Sagittarians are usually sociable creatures and the life and soul of any party, which might have them out drinking and partying regularly. Over-indulging can be a problem for some born under this sign and with the liver being one of the parts of the body that Sagittarians are associated with, hangovers could be particularly unpleasant for them, or at least that might be their excuse for staying in bed. Keeping a broad variety of friends will help a Sagittarian's social calendar have a healthier balance of partying and relaxation time. The invite for tea at a Taurean's house is just as important as the Leo friend that always has tickets for premiers or nightclub openings.

For Sagittarians that feel the Centaur running strongly inside of them, spending time outdoors will be of huge importance to their physical and mental health. For a sign that is constantly on the move like wildfire, taking a slow walk to soak up the wonders of Mother Nature could help soothe their racing mind. For city Sagittarians, reading their book in a park or signing up for an outdoor boot camp class could help bring them back to earth. Some Sagittarians may find that they have an affinity with horses and that the feeling of countryside air rushing past their cheeks gives them the greatest pleasure. If this sign is so inclined, horse riding will have the double benefit of bringing them joy and a level of fitness.

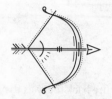

Sagittarius

. . . .

DAILY FORECASTS
for 2021

OCTOBER

. . . .

Friday 1st

You get some of your fire back today as the Moon drops into your travel sector. You're itching to get out and broaden your horizons. Look at breathing fresh life into your social groups. You may find that a new connection or invitation comes your way and excites your sense of adventure.

Saturday 2nd

Communications need to be measured and considered right now. You may be confronted with discussions that are multi-layered and complicated to understand. It's possible that you're pushy with your own opinion and stubborn when accepting another's. Hidden desires may be triggered and surface for healing.

Sunday 3rd

This morning you're in a steady, reliable and methodical mood. You may feel at a standstill but will work your way through this eventually. It will feel uncomfortable at first and you may have to deal with awkward people. Stay with the facts and you'll not go wrong.

Monday 4th

The Moon in your career sector helps you to stay grounded and on track. Uranus connects to nudge you out of a rut, and you may find the answer to a problem. It's tempting to drift off and ignore your duties, but you're professional and goal-orientated.

Tuesday 5th

You may overindulge and buy something for the home which is frivolous and expensive. Ideas of decluttering or a total make-over have been milling around your head recently and you may have taken the plunge already. Clearing up a part of your life is satisfying.

Wednesday 6th

A new moon in your social sector could be the start of a new way of relating to your wider groups. New energy comes in and excites you. Mars is connecting to make this Moon driven and assertive. Perhaps your groups are onto something big. Pluto also turns direct.

Thursday 7th

The harmonising Moon squares off with Pluto. Change is afoot whether you like it or not. There's much discussion, thought and research going on. You may like to join an activist movement which will bring about a much-needed change. The Moon enters your hidden sector just as Venus leaves it.

Friday 8th

The Sun and Mars are sitting together in your social sector. This is a time of high activity where egos may clash or combine to get things shifted. A rebellion may start now. The Moon in your hidden sector is rousing feelings you would usually keep to yourself.

Saturday 9th

Your emotions are focused on yourself as the Moon drops into your own sign and meets Venus. Putting yourself first is important now. No more accepting things and people who aren't good for you. Mercury and Mars meet too. Expect a lot of words and action that comes from the heart.

Sunday 10th

Saturn turns direct in your communications sector. The shackles are off and you can preach from your soapbox. It's likely that his retrograde taught you a thing or two about getting the right audience and being mindful when speaking. You're a force to be reckoned with now.

Monday 11th

You must put your own opinions to one side and listen carefully to the advice from an elder, leader or spiritual person. This will stand you in good stead in the near future. Jupiter, your ruler, is connecting to the Moon and has an important message for you.

Tuesday 12th

A gentle day comes as a relief to you. The Moon in your finance sector connects to Uranus so it's possible that you make an impulse buy. You may also see a new way to get through your mundane duties which will reap benefits in the long-term.

Wednesday 13th

You're getting closer to your true north but still need to clear the decks and make space. Start by listening to Venus who wants you to feel good about change. Letting something go need not be a heartache if it's done with love and compassion.

Thursday 14th

In your communications sector, the Moon meets newly direct Saturn. This may manifest as a meeting with a teacher or elder where you have to justify your recent actions. Open your mind, a fresh new lesson is about to start, and it comes from a brand new you.

Friday 15th

To verify Saturn's lessons, the Moon now meets Jupiter. Your ruler will turn direct this week but needs to ensure that your adventurous soul is ready. Truth and only truth will be acceptable now. You must throw away false teachings and flaky philosophies and make your own way.

Saturday 16th

Spending time with your tribe will be a pleasant activity this weekend. The Moon supports this with soft energy as you merge and connect with your loved ones. Simply allow yourself to go with the tides and appreciate the beauty of family. Celebrate the diversity within your family unit.

Sunday 17th

As the Moon meets Neptune and you enjoy detaching from problems, Jupiter turns direct. Your ruler blesses you with his gifts of optimism and joy. This can be a day where everyone chips in and gets a chore done or alternatively a family event becomes a party. Expect surprises today.

Monday 18th

Mercury turns direct. The pressure is lifting from your communications and social sectors. If you have put off signing a contract or making a travel plan, rest assured that you can now revisit these and forge ahead. This afternoon gives you the energy and motivation to soldier on.

Tuesday 19th

Your creative sector hosts the Moon and you're high-spirited. The future is clearer, and plans can be restarted. Mars is connecting to your ruler and you have the go-ahead to express yourself at all levels. Venus wishes you to speak from the heart and ask for what you desire now.

Wednesday 20th

There's a full moon in your creative sector. You may see something come to completion. A love affair is highlighted, as are children. It's possible that you're overwhelmed with something and your energy is drained as Mars is opposing the Moon.

Thursday 21st

You may come across a small stumbling block which will fuel your temper very quickly. This will feel like you've only just begun something on a high note and instantly you have run into problems. Stay calm, this isn't as bad as you first think it is.

Friday 22nd

Don't give up at the first hurdle. You have a moment where you just want to switch off and forget about everything. You're being hard on yourself and over-exaggerating the situation. This is a passing phase and will be over quickly. Don't jeopardise your potential now.

Saturday 23rd

If it's possible, spend today with someone who knows and understands you very well. You may wish to think and ruminate out loud. Thrashing out ideas and feelings about something with a lover may help to give you a better perspective. The Sun enters and illuminates your hidden sector.

Sunday 24th

The one thing you mustn't forget to do is to express your own needs. The Moon sits opposite Venus and you may be inclined to go along with another even if you don't feel right about it. Mercury is allowing you to speak freely with your social groups.

Monday 25th

Your dreams and visions might not be accessible to you but that doesn't stop you from discussing them. You may be overly assertive and feel self-righteous. Be careful that you don't brag or become a bore. Say your piece but prepare to hear another.

Tuesday 26th

You're emotionally inclined to think deeply and intensely today. It's likely that you cannot emotionally detach from your opinions. You may be defensive and protective of your own home, money and belief systems. Take some time alone today to recharge your batteries as you may be emotionally drained.

Wednesday 27th

The Moon opposes Pluto and that familiar nagging for change returns. You aren't ready to do this right now. Stay inside your comfort zone and don't let yourself be bullied or manipulated. You may need to switch off and close down again. See to your own emotional needs first.

Thursday 28th

Venus and Jupiter connect to make it possible for you to express yourself clearly. The Moon in your travel sector makes you outgoing and courageous. Short bursts are better than sustained effort today. Speak your mind truthfully then agree to draw a line under it for the sake of your energy.

Friday 29th

You must be very careful not to keep blowing your own trumpet today. Uranus the disruptor is connecting to the Moon and you may be so emotionally charged that you blow up in volcanic proportions. Surround yourself with your wider friendship groups and gather advice and wisdom.

Saturday 30th

Mars enters your hidden sector. This will have the effect of you being ruthless and brutal with your inner work. You may be very hard on yourself. The Sun is squaring off with Saturn which also confirms that you're working hard to bring out your shadow and heal it.

Sunday 31st

Concern yourself with daily chores as it will help take your mind off deeper issues. Take a break from the intense and do mundane work. Go through a messy drawer, do some admin or check your planner and schedules. Add some dates to your diary for treat times.

NOVEMBER
. . . .

Monday 1st

Today you may be trying to achieve harmony between your work and home life. You get an idea of changes to be made and how you might do this comfortably. Mercury helps you to think about which contacts are good for you and will help you grow.

Tuesday 2nd

Your social network takes up your mind and heart space. The Moon meets the point of destiny and you're pulled towards making choices which will feed your soul. New and exciting causes stimulate your need to do something worthwhile for the greater good of the wider world.

Wednesday 3rd

You have a heart to heart with yourself and you may try separating logic from emotion. This is not easy to do. Pluto is still asking for you to end something and this could be a project you have a lot of emotional investment in. You will find a way in time.

Thursday 4th

The Moon enters your hidden sector and meets Mars. You may feel some anxiety and tension. This will become a full moon and give you some insight or deeper introspection. This is likely to be uncomfortable so take time to process these new feelings and epiphanies.

Friday 5th

There's a lot of highly charged energy for you to deal with.
The Sun in your hidden sector antagonises Uranus. You may
see shadow material surfacing and experience many triggers.
Mercury enters your private hidden sector. This will help you
to dig as deep as you need to find the answers.

Saturday 6th

The Moon enters your sign and your emotions settle down
a little. Venus is in your finance and values sector and making a
great connection to Mercury. Between the two of them, they will
ensure that you understand your self-worth and the process of
healing you are going through.

Sunday 7th

You might feel that you have lost sight of your dreams and as
if your inner compass does not seem to be calibrated very well.
Your ruler, Jupiter, asks that you stay positive and look at
things from a different angle, just for today. How does it feel
to observe yourself from the outside?

Monday 8th

Doing the hard work of introspection is beginning to pay off.
It's likely that you've surprised yourself with how much you've
learned about your inner defaults already. Mars is driving you
on and Mercury is sharing the information he finds with you.

Tuesday 9th

The Moon meets Pluto. You have a chance to recycle something or put it in the refuse bin once and for all. This may be a positive death and rebirth of values you once lived by and have now realised don't serve you anymore.

Wednesday 10th

Mercury and Mars meet up and become a source of strength to you. Saturn is watching how you deal with situations that may require you to be Saturn-like. You will need to be firm and fair and put healthy boundaries in place to protect your energy and vulnerability right now.

Thursday 11th

The Moon in your communications sector meets Jupiter. Recent feelings may now feel bigger and ready to burst. You're ready for these to be exposed. Speaking your truth may upset someone or interrupt your daily routine. This will be brief, and you can deal with it easily.

Friday 12th

Today the Sun makes a connection to Neptune that helps you see things with a little more clarity. The whole picture will not be revealed just yet, but some of the fog is lifting. This will make you pause and take note before you proceed any further. Venus will bring you balance.

Saturday 13th

Let the Moon guide you into enjoying some family time.
With your tribe, you may be able to align your inner compass
once more. Listen to your heart as the Moon meets Neptune.
Be still and patient. Refrain from spilling your secrets today as
this could have unwanted effects.

Sunday 14th

You're much blessed as the Sun and Moon are in sync.
Your ego and conscious mind are in touch with your
emotions and you feel happy. This afternoon your creative
side comes out and you're able to reach out to others and
be an example to them.

Monday 15th

Don't let anything knock you back. It may be that you've come
across an obstruction or unforeseen problem. Talk to people
about this, don't try solving it on your own as you will become
frustrated. You need help from a professional or someone in
your wider groups.

Tuesday 16th

Weird energy has you thinking about endings and beginnings
but in different ways. The Sun in your hidden sector may
make you feel ready for action, but the Moon has an emotional
connection that you're not ready to cut just yet. Take note of
how this is triggering you and sleep on it.

Wednesday 17th

The Moon shifts into your health and duties sector. This time of the month is useful if you need to distract yourself from deeper issues. However, Mars in your hidden sector is facing off with Uranus and that can only mean trouble. Stress may get to you.

Thursday 18th

The best thing you can do today is to lie low. If it's possible, speak to no one and stay home protecting your energy. Pick up a fantasy novel or binge-watch a TV show. The planetary energy is far too unstable and can tip you over the edge. Stay safe.

Friday 19th

A full moon in your heath and duties sector may be the culmination of a health problem. This is like a spotlight on how you get through your day and how much you look after yourself. You may have experienced burn out. Venus tries to soothe you today, allow her to do so.

Saturday 20th

You need a close friend or lover to talk to this weekend. It will be helpful for you to simply talk and talk. You need to be heard and validated. Find someone with whom you can reveal your darker sides and not be judged. Some of your inner thoughts need to be revealed now.

Sunday 21st

If today feels like you have lost your way again, be assured that this is just a quickly passing Moon phase. Be good to yourself and breathe deeply. A lover or best friend may have remedies or solutions that are new and useful for you. Talking therapy is the best.

Monday 22nd

The Sun enters your sign, so this is your birthday month. Happy Birthday! Venus and Mars are making a good connection enabling you to find the warrior heart within you. You will do the right thing and make plenty of time for yourself now.

Tuesday 23rd

The Moon and Venus are opposing each other, and you have guilty feelings about being too self-indulgent. This is not the case, you're currently doing a lot of deep work and this needs time and self-love. Carry on doing the right thing for you.

Wednesday 24th

Mercury is finishing up his time in your psyche. It's crucial now that you take care of all the pearls he has discovered in your darkest places. His underworld research has brought you information that you can throw to Pluto the next time he asks.

Thursday 25th

Mercury enters your sign and meets the point of past lessons. This is a great opportunity to let him drop something in there and let it go for good. Mars and Venus are supporting this and giving you masculine strength and feminine compassion to lovingly release some baggage.

Friday 26th

Today you're brave and outgoing. Slight reservations prevent you from being the truth-seeking Sagittarius you are, but your optimism still shines through. You may wish to look at some study options which will help with your soul work and bring you into touch with like-minded people.

Saturday 27th

Your sense of calm returns and you're much more centred. Mercury has unearthed your treasure, shown it to you and discarded the waste. Today you may think about a thorough detox of your body and mind. A spiritual retreat or group could do wonders for you. Try meditation or yoga, too.

Sunday 28th

The Moon opposes Neptune and you defer from entering the fantasy world he is offering. Stay on task as you declutter and cleanse yourself. You may have a revelation or two as you do so. Good food and company can help to keep you grounded.

Monday 29th

Mercury is silent in your own sign. Remain centred and listen to his messages. Your social groups may now offer a way that you can achieve your soul desires. Mars is still the driving force in your psyche and connects to Neptune to recalibrate your inner compass.

Tuesday 30th

Today there is lovely energy for you to access and work with. Venus and Neptune connect to show you the true value in your personal quest. Mercury and the Sun are receiving a lesson from Saturn. Your ego and essence are becoming more authentic as you learn more about your inner workings. Well done, this is fantastic.

DECEMBER

·····················

Wednesday 1st

Neptune turns direct. Finally, you'll be able to grasp hold of your inner compass and let it guide you. The Moon dips into your hidden sector and you may find that you're looking around there and evaluating the job Mercury has just facilitated for you.

Thursday 2nd

Today may give you a test of some kind. The Moon sits opposite the disruptive Uranus and you may resent any or all things that appear to obstruct your dreams and visions. Sit tight and bite your lip, this will pass as quickly as it has come up.

Friday 3rd

When the Moon meets Mars in your hidden sector you become fiercely protective of your private life. This could cause you to detach and refuse to listen to important people. You may now begin to do things simply for the sake of not conforming to others' expectations of you.

Saturday 4th

A new moon arrives in your sign. This will give you the green light you've been seeking to go ahead and follow your heart. Mercury gives you the itinerary and map. You already have the compass. Play by the rules and you won't fail. Set all your personal goals now.

Sunday 5th

Jupiter has a say now. He connects to the Moon in a helpful way and fills you with optimism and motivation. There's much for you to learn, discover and experience. Keep your fire alive as it's your driving force. Keep your eyes on the goal.

Monday 6th

The Moon is in your finance and values sector. You might find that you turn to the financial aspect of attaining your goals. Mars and Pluto assist with this as they are both concerned with money. Be studious and leave no stone unturned. Be responsible and think before you act.

Tuesday 7th

Pluto hosts the Moon and you may be looking at taxes, bank accounts or regular subscriptions. There may be some that are out of date or due for renewal. A back-up of resources may be required and is highly recommended. Make the necessary enquiries this afternoon.

Wednesday 8th

Be very patient. Once again you may find that there are obstacles in your way. Mars and Uranus are making you irritable and you're likely to throw a tantrum. Take it easy and ask around, there are others out there who can offer words of wisdom without you having to rebel.

. . . .

Thursday 9th

It's time that you looked at the legalities of your dreams. Jupiter reminds you that law and order are part of the truth you desire. Let nothing trip you up. Stay calm. This afternoon you may be more idealistic. Keep one foot on the ground if you can.

Friday 10th

Today you may get a surprising piece of support from a family member. An innovative way of solving a problem may come to you and you make a small breakthrough. You're more open to advice so listen well, as it may come from an unlikely source.

Saturday 11th

The Moon meets Neptune as Venus meets Pluto. This influence will serve you very well. You're focused on your dreams and visions and able to factor in the financial consequences. Venus also helps to make any change go the way you desire. You may feel a major shift.

Sunday 12th

Get your creative juices flowing as there's something that needs your attention. You may be asked your unique opinion on something and the ideas come flowing freely. Venus and Pluto are still together bringing in the money and letting unnecessary things go. This is all good energy.

Monday 13th

Two planets change signs. Mercury enters your finance and values sector and becomes your money manager. Watch what is offered to you now. Mars enters your sign and will give you all the fire you need to march your way into your future. Buying and selling may be an option.

Tuesday 14th

You may have a moment where you're not looking after number one today. This may derail you a little. However, as the Moon enters your health and duties sector it gets easier to ask for what you want. A reshuffle of your duties may be in order now.

Wednesday 15th

The Moon meets Uranus and you could be in for a surprise. This could be a visit from a ghost of the past. Saturn is watching to see if your personal boundaries are strong and healthy enough to deal with this in a respectful manner.

Thursday 16th

After a small hiccup, you're back on track, making changes, clearing the decks and putting yourself first. The weekend is lining up for some time with a lover or best friend. Prepare now and get all your chores out of the way. You'll want to free up plenty of time.

Friday 17th

You're in the mood to talk until the small hours. Pick your partner and enjoy time together or an early festive celebration. Mars in your sign sits opposite the Moon and you may be energised enough to dance or talk all night. Make sure that your partner is too.

Saturday 18th

Venus will turn retrograde today. This is a period of forty days in which you could possibly see an ex-lover return, relationships end or a lack of self-care. As she is in your finance and values sector it will likely manifest as money problems or low self-esteem.

Sunday 19th

A full moon hangs in your relationship sector and connects to your ruler. This is beneficial for lovers and those who like to learn, study and share their understanding. What did you begin in this area six months ago? Has something come to fruition now? You're possibly feeling a bit protective of your relationships this evening.

Monday 20th

As the festive season arrives, take some time to gather in your favourite foods and activities. Mothers and fathers play a big role. Look at your defence mechanisms as they may trigger some unnecessary feelings in you. You may be told off like a child today.

Tuesday 21st

Today's the winter solstice. The longest night serves to remind you to give gratitude for the long days and to preserve your energy throughout the winter months. You may see a power struggle or some miscommunication. Enjoy the solstice fire energy now as it suits your outgoing manner.

Wednesday 22nd

The Sun settles into your finance and value sector. This will help you to see where you sometimes undervalue yourself. Remember this when Venus retrograde effect comes upon you. You are worthy of receiving grace and must keep your fire burning to guide others. The only way is up.

Thursday 23rd

Jupiter is saying goodbye to your communications sector. He will now spend a whole year bringing luck, joy and optimism to your family. Step into this next year with your ruler bestowing his good cheer all around. The festivities have come early for you and your tribe.

Friday 24th

You may need to get your serious mind working today. The Moon passes into your career sector and this is where you are methodical, meticulous and do everything by the rules. You will see tension building around you, but this is natural. Take the lead if you must.

Saturday 25th

Venus has retrograded back to meet Pluto. This festive day will not be without some power struggles and manipulation. You have likely overspent and it has come back to haunt you. Forget about your personal dreams today, go with the flow and join in the collective family dream.

Sunday 26th

You have complete control over the festive proceedings.
You may even be hosting them. This afternoon, however,
you're more inclined to spread some cheer with your social
groups, even if it's just online. You tell a family member or
two about your new goals and have a pleasant time doing so.

Monday 27th

Today the major rush of the season is feeling more balanced.
You still have energy and can compensate for older family
members and friends who have run out of steam. Be respectful
and helpful to those who may need you to do odd jobs or simply
require your presence.

Tuesday 28th

You may start to feel the strain. It's possible that you
experience that ghost from the past re-entering your life.
It's tempting to renew this connection, but you must have a
serious think about it first. What can it offer you? Why did
it leave you before, and what has changed to bring it back?
Do this when the Moon enters your hidden sector tonight.

Wednesday 29th

Today is another test for you. The Moon opposes Uranus who is
upsetting things in your health and duties sector. It's possible
that you see a minor health problem after overdoing the festive
treats. You will need to slow down. Detach and take time alone
if you need to.

Thursday 30th

When you're alone, you secretly delight in the achievements of this year. You've worked hard and you are pleased with the results you have seen. Mercury has met Pluto for the first time since he was in your psyche and today he's disposing of the last of the garbage. See if you can feel this release and watch it go with love and compassion.

Friday 31st

The Moon is in your sign and you will be the life and soul of any New Year's Eve party. Mars gives you the energy you need for a fun time. Say goodbye to this year and give thanks for the lessons it has brought you. Then celebrate all you have accomplished and all you have to look forward to in the coming year.

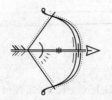

Sagittarius

. . . .

DAILY FORECASTS
for 2022

JANUARY

Saturday 1st
Happy New Year and welcome to 2022. Aim for a relaxing day as your own needs could clash with family matters and make you irritable. A little brain fog could be the result of overindulgence. Be prepared for a late surprise or an addition to your resources today. This year could see an increase in your values and finances.

Sunday 2nd
A new moon gives you the chance to set intentions and goals regarding what you own and what is important to you. This might mean that you are building on something which will raise your status and self-esteem. It's time to get networking and see what's available to you.

Monday 3rd
There could be an antagonist from the past; maybe a lover who is trying to make their presence known. Control issues and power struggles could surface. Take a good look at what you need to cut ties with and work on this now. Think outside the box for a solution to problems.

Tuesday 4th
Your mind and heart are in sync today. Ideas flow through you but may not all be easy to implement. However, rise to the challenge and try not to get irritated. Speak to elders or others who've experienced this before you. A valuable lesson is there to learn today.

Wednesday 5th

You could be extra motivated today. There is a plan hatching in your mind and you could be keen to get things moving now that the holiday season is over. This could be something you put your heart into and work hard for. Sustain this if you can.

Thursday 6th

Today can be joyous and filled with optimism. Perhaps you have big plans which involve your family. Jupiter in your family zone can indicate new additions or a general sense of wellbeing and opportunity. Your search for spiritual truth and knowledge might begin at home or at your roots.

Friday 7th

Your energy could wane today, but don't despair. This is temporary and is a chance for you to check in with your inner compass and ensure that where you're heading is absolutely in alignment with your core values. Let no one dictate your worth today. Watch out for subtle manipulation tactics.

Saturday 8th

Today is a good day to begin a new project. You can be driven and excited to present this to the outside world. Romantic and creative pursuits are favoured now. Speaking your mind is easy as it will come also from the heart. You may be more open to suggestions.

Sunday 9th

Be very careful today as a pull from the past could be upsetting. You might experience this as a money or possessions issue which someone is trying to take from you. Hold tight and be the better person. A mature attitude will win. Don't compromise your own values at all.

Monday 10th

You could be reluctant to do what's necessary and make a permanent ending. If you find that your courage is wavering, think about the space you will have for new growth when you have cleared the debris from the past. Conversations can be upsetting or reveal a harsh truth today.

Tuesday 11th

Challenging energy can make this a rough day. You may have too many things to do for others and can be left feeling resentful. This phase will pass, but you will need to avoid unnecessary outbursts. Plan a nice meal or a simple pleasure for yourself at the end of the day.

Wednesday 12th

Your spirits may be lifted today, and you can manage little problems responsibly. A ghost from the past may not bother you or you find a solution which eliminates this irritation in the kindest possible way. Indulge in something which makes you feel good and on form.

Thursday 13th

As the Moon drops into your relationship zone, you may feel that you need comfort and support from your partner. You must try not to project your issues now as you will come across as selfish and inconsiderate. Meet a partner on common ground and give equally to one another.

Friday 14th

Mercury turns retrograde today. As this happens in your communications zone you will need to be extra careful and clear in conversation. Back up all your devices and double-check travel plans. Refrain from committing to anything or signing contracts during this time. Instead, go over anything you've worked on recently.

Saturday 15th

Your energy could be low today, but you could use this opportunity to relax with your partner and let them take care of you. This afternoon you may wish to stay in your comfort zone. You may also feel vulnerable or attacked. Nurture yourself and lie low for the day.

Sunday 16th

Be on the alert today for an opportunity to make a significant change. This may include finances or your self-worth. You may receive some enlightenment and feel positive about the future. However, tricky energy suggests that you could also be susceptible to rash actions or harsh words with someone who is bothering you.

Monday 17th

Get a grip on what you want to achieve with your family this year. A full moon may bring things to light which highlight your security needs. Delving too far into the darker side of life might have unearthed deep-seated emotions of safety and protection.

Tuesday 18th

Uranus turns direct today. Any turbulence regarding health issues or the way you serve others may begin to settle. You can be more outgoing and playful now. Use your voice to explore the wider world. What appeals to your inner child may be good for your soul and help you grow.

Wednesday 19th

Try not to be too fixed in your views this morning. A teacher may try to help you with their own experience, but you could be too stubborn to consider other options. Let a wise person offer their guidance and think about it for a while. Disregarding anything will be foolish.

Thursday 20th

You can be more driven to achieve your goals today. Using a more methodical approach can help you work through problems and achieve results. Go through everything and search for the details. You may be showcasing your abilities today, so make a good impression. Try and remember to keep focused on the little things.

Friday 21st

Hard work will pay off now as you can be more determined to problem-solve and get rid of annoyances. Earthy energy can help you to stay grounded and stick to the job in hand. Your self-esteem will benefit greatly from thinking outside the box and being inventive.

Saturday 22nd

Morning brain fog will be cleared if you continue to do practical or physical work today. Applying yourself this way can leave the evening free to enjoy social time with groups of friends. You could benefit from connecting with like-minded folk and feeding from their encouragement and support.

Sunday 23rd

You may feel an urge to complete something which is important to you. However, this feeling may also be your eagerness to start a new project. Mercury is in the heart of the Sun and receiving new downloads. It's your job to listen and not to act today. Think of this as preparation time.

Monday 24th

Now is the time to start something which can raise your status or improve your finances. Over the next month, you may be single-minded and acutely focused on achieving your goals. However, as these may be long-term goals, you will need a plan with small steady steps for success.

Tuesday 25th

As the Moon drops into your most private zone, you could find that you are more introspective than usual. You may be mulling over many issues at once. Family members can be your support team now as old conditioning and habits might be surfacing and are not helpful.

Wednesday 26th

Mercury retrogrades into your finance and values zone. Perhaps there is something here which needs to be reviewed. Research all possibilities and you may discover information you previously missed. There may still be an issue with an ex-lover or person from your past to deal with. Use tact and diplomacy but stay aligned to your inner compass.

Thursday 27th

It may be obvious what needs to be removed from your life today. You could wake knowing exactly what to do. Discarding old baggage can be good for your soul. This may make you feel more like yourself again, but could rub up against family issues.

Friday 28th

Your sense of responsibility to yourself is high now and this can fuel you through your day. You may find that family members or your own dreams need to be given space or time. It could be hard to see through an old illusion or make sense of other people's behaviour.

Saturday 29th

Venus turns direct now, and you may get some relief from
irritations from the past. Unfinished business can be concluded
and respectfully let go once and for all. You may feel this
positive change in your health and wellbeing too. You can be
more determined to aim for the stars.

Sunday 30th

Your heart may feel the pull of what you've recently let go
of. It's okay to grieve for what something once meant to you,
just don't dwell on it. You may be too fixated on this today to
enjoy anything else. You should do something just for you this
evening.

Monday 31st

Your mind may be doing overtime while you sleep, but you
would be wise to pay attention to your dreams. Clues may
appear in all forms and you should take note. Conversations
may also be enlightening and unusual. Be inventive and
open-minded to whatever crosses your path today.

FEBRUARY

....

Tuesday 1st

Today's new moon is a great opportunity to make plans which involve researching, learning and being a part of the wider world. Which groups interest you? What more can you do to contribute? Just think about this for now and wait until Mercury turns direct before taking any action.

Wednesday 2nd

You can be more flexible now, which makes you feel good. Families may drain your finances and resources, but this will be temporary, and you may have fun doing so. Let your home of origin be a source of empathy, compassion and connection. Go with the flow and be inspired today.

Thursday 3rd

This is a great day for impulsive action which pays off. You could be taking steps towards better self-care or have a great idea which can boost your finances and your self-worth. Family members can be encouraging and optimistic. Indulge in something which makes you feel special. Good food and company can suffice.

Friday 4th

Mercury turns direct now. You can begin to think about new projects which involve networking or learning new skills. Notice how aligned you feel with your core values. Your motivation and will to succeed drives you on and you could be seriously impressing a superior. It's your day to shine.

Saturday 5th

Be careful not to overdo it today. You could be at risk of burnout. Ensure that you schedule in some downtime or space to let off steam. You could transfer your enthusiasm to your romantic and creative pursuits and still come away a winner.

Sunday 6th

Be sure to back up any grand gestures today. You may be back-pedalling if your mouth has run away with you. Keep a low flame burning under your romantic relationship, but take caution when expressing your needs as they may be in conflict with a partner's. Appease yourself with a treat this evening.

Monday 7th

Great energy can be uplifting, so ensure that you continue to strive for your personal goals. This earthy energy is grounding and can help you to keep things real. Enjoy what you have today and refrain from dreaming or thinking up new plans. Hard work and dedication will bring results.

Tuesday 8th

You could battle between your emotional needs and your busy mind today. Do what's necessary before thinking about your own goals. There'll be time to dream this evening when you can think about your basic needs and take care of your mundane duties with satisfaction.

Wednesday 9th

The future beckons and you might look at how you serve others and what comes back to you. You might be more inquisitive and indecisive, but partner time can help you to focus your mind or at least let you look at all your options. Inspiring conversations could give you a lot to think about.

Thursday 10th

Don't worry about things too much today. It's possible that you have overloaded your mind with needless worries. Things will look bigger than they actually are. A wise counsellor can help you to recognise your own limitations and stop your dreams from getting out of hand and unachievable.

Friday 11th

Use your intuition now. You could get an insight or revelation into what your new mission should be. This is possibly about your status, career, finances and values. Take on board any advice you're given and file it away for future use. Plan for a weekend of feeding your soul's needs.

Saturday 12th

The celestial lovers, Mars and Venus, are getting close in your finances and values zone. This is a great sign that you can use to plan how to get what you need. This might be a long-term goal, but the energy is there for you to access and plan accordingly.

Sunday 13th

You could have a small crisis today and self-doubt might creep in. However, this is an old thought process which you have outgrown and is no longer serving you. Realign with your inner compass and see how it has matured. Your personal goals require self-love and nurturing to evolve.

Monday 14th

There may be something outstanding which needs attention today. This could be an issue which you have bypassed unintentionally or put off. See to it now because the time is right for manifesting your desires, and you need to be ready for action. See what you can compost or transmute into something more useful.

Tuesday 15th

You could feel quite impatient now, but you must hold tight a little longer. Use this time to plan for your journey ahead. Try not to limit yourself or to breach boundaries. You must recognise that barriers are there for a reason and they will keep you safe.

Wednesday 16th

Under a full moon, Mars and Venus meet. You might notice that you feel confident and that your leadership qualities are activated. Keep your head held high and step boldly into the next phase of manifesting all that you wish for yourself. You could be checking the details this evening.

Thursday 17th

This evening you could be exhausted and need to wind down a little. However, this goes against your nature and you might keep pushing or working late. You could be more optimistic about a new adventure and see this as a quest for truth and connection with the wider world.

Friday 18th

A willingness to serve can be helpful in the workplace, but don't let yourself be taken for granted. You may be at risk of diverging from your inner compass. As the Sun enters your family zone, keep in mind that what you do affects your entire family.

Saturday 19th

You might be in the mood to socialise and have some fun with your interest groups or friendship circles. A light-hearted time with like-minded people can be good for you today. Conversations can be inspirational and innovative, promoting a sense of wellbeing within you and others. Enjoy a night off and relax.

Sunday 20th

You could be feeling a little unbalanced today, but this may simply be because you wish to get out and work on your personal goals. Take a day off while you can and don't beat yourself up for it. As long as you're being responsible, time off will be beneficial.

Monday 21st

The window is still open for you to activate your dream life. Masculine and feminine energy are combined for you to approach this with compassion and strength. Drop down into your psyche today and pull out the gold that's in the shadows. There could be some healing to do to become whole.

Tuesday 22nd

Deep investigation of your inner workings is part of this journey. You might find it disturbing and discover things that you have hidden for a long time. Let them see the light and you might be surprised by how you can manage these things with maturity.

Wednesday 23rd

You know that something from the past has held you back and needs to be dealt with. This could be as simple as letting a grievance go. It may be an issue around jealousy or being hurt by someone. Once you have recognised that it is detrimental to your growth, you can heal.

Thursday 24th

Today you are raring to go and your busy mind is eager to make the right connections and enquiries. You could be joining the dots and piecing together information. If an issue looks too big to manage, leave it for now and come back again with fresh eyes.

Friday 25th

Today you might feel that your inner compass is adrift. This will pass and is a sign that you have more pressing things to take care of. The nitty-gritty of everyday life or your career must take precedence now. Do the right things and there will be time to dream later.

Saturday 26th

Better energy suggests that you can follow your path whilst maintaining your emotional and spiritual connection to others. You may even find your soul family amongst your interest groups. Take a leap of faith today and step into a new phase of growth and abundance. Your ruler, Jupiter, will support you.

Sunday 27th

This is a great day for feeling sure that you're on the right track. The summit of the mountain you're about to climb may seem daunting, but know that you've equipped yourself with the right allies and resources for the journey. Stand tall and be proud of yourself.

Monday 28th

Don't listen to your inner critic today. You're doing just fine. You might be tempted to do something rash which could spoil your progress so far. Give yourself a talking to this evening and vow not to undo your good work with impulsive actions and poorly thought out plans.

MARCH

· · · · · · · · · · · · · · · · · ·

Tuesday 1st

Make sure that you're doing the best things for your body. If you find that you're exhausting yourself by appeasing others, your health could suffer. Remember to factor in time to enjoy simple pleasures and your health will improve. Good food and company or physical exercise could be just the thing for you.

Wednesday 2nd

A new moon is a chance to set goals and intentions around your family of origin, your personal dreams and need for privacy. Great changes are on the way and you could be anticipating these with a mature and responsible attitude. Your heart is expanding with big hopes.

Thursday 3rd

Your inner compass gets your attention today and you could feel perfectly aligned. This is a positive day and can bring in all sorts of good luck. The trick is to really know what you want and make it achievable. Out with the old and in with the new.

Friday 4th

Fiery energy inspires you to create, get romantic or begin a new project. This can feel so good that you might overdo it and need to slim it down again later. Keep it simple. You can be more playful now and at least make a list of plans for the weekend ahead.

Saturday 5th

This is another day filled with good fortune and opportunity. Your ruler, Jupiter, is visited by the Sun and is charged up for the year ahead. The focus will be on family, home and your roots. With Mars and Venus still travelling together your approach can be driven, compassionate and even-tempered.

Sunday 6th

Communications can be fruitful today. If there is something you desire, speak up and it could easily come your way. Remember that in order to make room for new growth, you need to clear some space. You might find that this occurs naturally today but may not be easy for you.

Monday 7th

You might be tempted to act irrationally today but by lunchtime you see sense. Your service is needed, and mundane duties take up your day. This is looked upon favourably by family members, but you must ensure that they understand your limits, or you could be taken for granted.

Tuesday 8th

You may be closer to reaching your ideal state of living than you think. A tricky conversation might derail you but will ultimately prove to be a catalyst for a much-needed change. As the Moon moves into your partner zone, wonder and awe can be the topics of discussion.

Wednesday 9th

With four planets in your communication zone, you might find that your busy mind has no anchor and your thoughts are scattered. However, you may also be full to the brim with ideas, concepts and things you'd like to explore. Interest groups and friendships can be sources of inspiration.

Thursday 10th

Today you must simply get on with the daily grind. You could feel irritable and slightly resentful as your time is taken up by others. There's no time to dream today, so you must simply attend to your responsibilities. This will be satisfying in itself as your compliance will be noticed.

Friday 11th

Your safety and protection needs matter now. You might think that by going off into a deep, dark fantasy world, you're protecting your energy, but be sure to understand that others are there to support you too. Your intuition is high now and you can communicate any concerns to your family.

Saturday 12th

Do something adventurous today. This should be easy for you, but you may wish to stay closer to home to do it. Emotionally, you may be in a good place and can explore life's mysteries from the safety of your home. Stay open for anything which could expand your mind.

Sunday 13th

Take a good look at your inner compass today. There is a possibility that any misconceptions or confusion could clear away today and make your route more obvious. You could be more protective of your own possessions and finances and may have trouble sharing with others. Don't get too controlling and self-righteous.

Monday 14th

Keep a low profile today. Tricky energy could make you argumentative and problems appear larger than they are. You might not be in a good frame of mind and won't suffer fools. Conflict or volatile behaviour is possible. If compromise isn't possible, walk away from potentially challenging situations.

Tuesday 15th

You could still be tense and irritable. Dealing with authority figures can make you feel worse. You would do best to attend to your responsibilities and duties and leave anything else for another day. You could realise your own limitations today which can make you resentful. This mood will pass.

Wednesday 16th

Today you could be much more inclined to do administration work. Paperwork such as filing and sorting can be soothing and restore your mood. Your role at work might require you to be meticulous and check every detail. This is something you can apply your mind to and change your mood.

Thursday 17th

Minor problems could surface from within your family.
These may impact your productivity but can be dealt with.
Use the power of speech to persuade others to think outside
the box to solve issues. This might prove to be exciting as
well as useful. Genius thinking suits you.

Friday 18th

A full moon could highlight a completion or target met in the
workplace or your status. This is down to your way of drawing
on emotional needs and being flexible. Plan a social event for
the weekend and reconnect with your soul tribe as they are
your safe place to let off steam.

Saturday 19th

You have a better sense of balance and harmony now. This may
be a result of using your free time for fun and light-hearted
connection. However, you might have to go along with the
majority today and follow their suggestions for activities.
You will probably enjoy it eventually.

Sunday 20th

The spring equinox arrives and brings you an opportunity to
sit, contemplate and ponder your next move. The anticipation
in the air might be exhilarating, but you must choose your
time to make a move. This could be a new romance or creative
project that you're passionate about.

Monday 21st

Listen carefully to your inner voice today. You may have a revelation which can lead to big things. Alternatively, other energy suggests that you could be tuning into your inner critic instead. Press pause again and sit still. Wait until your mood lifts before you initiate anything new as you may need clarity.

Tuesday 22nd

Your dreams may be more accessible today, but a lot of deep thought and introspection is needed first. Once again, you're being asked to let go of something and make space. This evening you may be more fired up but could also be at risk of acting rashly.

Wednesday 23rd

Today is much better for acting in the most positive way possible. You could be more sensible and methodical. Do what is right for you and your inner compass will show you that you have made the best choice. Talking with family members could help you to work it through mentally.

Thursday 24th

Another anxious day could mean that nothing gets done. Again, this is a passing phase and is reminding you not to rush into anything. Plans are best adhered to and rules shouldn't be broken to gain a quick fix. This is a long journey and you must take the proper steps.

Friday 25th

You could be torn between getting busy or following a schedule. This might seem tedious but is necessary to ensure you stay on the right path. By evening you could have some ingenious thoughts which should be noted for future use. Radical doesn't always mean wrong.

Saturday 26th

Things might be fitting into place better today. You are more optimistic and see the sense in taking things slowly. Mercury asks if there is anything urgent you need to get off your chest regarding your family and roots. Merge with those who know you best and you may be supported.

Sunday 27th

Communications may seem like a hotline today. Ideas flow and verbal exchanges can be enlightening. However, you must also be discerning and look at all the information offered. There could be something which doesn't feel right. If this is the case, it's not meant for you, so leave it behind.

Monday 28th

There is great, positive energy for you to access today. This can give you a chance to show that you mean business. Connections made via the airwaves can be what you need to put a plan into action. You can remain responsible and respectful whilst thriving within your limitations.

Tuesday 29th

An emotional and sensitive Moon means that your intuition can be higher than usual. This can be a good time for connecting with family members or spiritual support groups. Go with the flow today, but do so with compassion. Your typical fiery and impulsive nature needs to be calmed and steadied right now.

Wednesday 30th

You have countless blessings waiting for you today. What will you do with them? A midweek celebration may be in order. Dream big and reach for the stars. Your inner compass and ruling planet are in sync and are wishing the absolute best for you. Make the most of this.

Thursday 31st

It's possible that you're activating your plans now. These could include a new romance, and this is well favoured. The past no longer bothers you and you've made enough space for something beautiful to grow. Keep tending that flame of inspiration, desire and passion and it could warm your whole being.

APRIL
. . . .

Friday 1st
A new moon to begin this month is the green light you've been waiting for. Activate, initiate and press go on your most creative projects including love and self-expression. You can be a force to be reckoned with if you heed this moment and make a game plan.

Saturday 2nd
You can be your most generous and inspiring self today. If you play it right, you could be rewarded with simple pleasures and things you enjoy doing this evening. Don't let a small doubt spoil your day as this is easily resolved with the attitude that change is how growth happens.

Sunday 3rd
Mercury is in the heart of the Sun today receiving new downloads. It's your job to listen intently to subtle messages and symbols. You may discover your muse now and creativity could flow through you in abundance. Shout out your intentions and make your voice heard. Be a leader and light the way.

Monday 4th
Returning to the working week might seem dull today as you don't want to be put in a box. Know that there are boundaries to adhere to in parts of life, and once these have been acknowledged, the rest of the time is yours. Be practical and do your chores.

Tuesday 5th

Conversations can be fraught with misunderstanding and antagonism. You could feel undermined or blocked. Partner time can be a source of comfort, but be careful not to project your angst onto someone you care about. Your family life will experience more harmony and beauty in the coming month.

Wednesday 6th

Bright ideas continue to flow through you and now they're enhanced by research. You could be studying or learning something about a partner which can lead to a new level of relating. Conversations can be light and playful now, so enjoy this downtime before getting serious again.

Thursday 7th

A sleepless night may be the result of a busy mind. If you border on negative thinking, find your safety net and comfort your inner child. You may be using coping methods which once served you as a child but are now outdated and useless. Listen to your intuition. What does your soul need?

Friday 8th

You have the opportunity to dream big again today. Just be careful not to pursue a line of enquiry which is an illusion. If it seems too good to be true, it probably isn't true. However, if something comes up which can be beneficial, grab it with both hands.

Saturday 9th

Today you may find that your need for security clashes with your desire to get on and create. Allow yourself more time to feel protected and nurtured. Rely on another person for a change. You may need to find a confidante to share your dreams and aspirations with.

Sunday 10th

You've had enough of being swaddled and cared for. This can be stifling and today you may break free. What you may not realise is that knowing you're safe and loved is the basis for your ability to explore, be bold and brave. Your foundations are secure, and you can spread your wings.

Monday 11th

There are more blessings for you today. Family could provide you with love and laughter, generosity and dreams. You could find that this enhancement leads you to a fantasy island and together with your kin you can build something which pleases you all. A shared dream can be exciting.

Tuesday 12th

You may have to stand your ground and make your voice count today. There could be opposition to long-term plans concerning travel, learning or connecting with different cultures. Perhaps a holiday may need to be taken closer to home. Work issues might play on your mind this evening.

Wednesday 13th

Although you're doing the right thing and sticking to your guns, you could be up against someone in your family or home of origin who is rocking the boat. Practical measures may need to be taken. You could be working at home on a DIY project which freshens things up.

Thursday 14th

More restrictions from family can make you tired and drain your energy for your job. You might need to be direct and assertive. It could be that a shared dream is already falling apart. Reserve your right to pull out of something which isn't working the way you hoped.

Friday 15th

Get ready for a sociable weekend. There may be a lot going on at home and an escape with like-minded friends and acquaintances could be your remedy. With four planets in your family zone, home may be an overwhelming place to be right now. Keep it real and amicable.

Saturday 16th

A full moon can show you who your friends are. If there's been any issues, they will now come to a head and be exposed. This could go two ways. It can be a positive event with equality and harmony, or it could show where the weak links are in your collective.

Sunday 17th

A quiet day might do you good. You could have a lot of introspection to do and being alone with your thoughts might give you a chance to process recent events. The deepest parts of your psyche hold hidden treasures and you may need to bring them into the light.

Monday 18th

Your mind may be mulling over old issues concerning jealousy, suspicion and deep hurt. Old wounds need to be healed and not picked open again. Irritability can distract you from your work, so try to deal with one thing at a time. Your inner compass supports any healing you need to do.

Tuesday 19th

As the Moon drops into your sign, you can feel more like yourself. However, your personal energy may not be up to your usual drive and enthusiasm. Be open and flexible to rearranging your chores depending on your energy levels. Don't do any more than you need to.

Wednesday 20th

Today you could experience considerable confrontation with family members. As hard as you try to use compassion, empathy and understanding, you resent being involved in problems that aren't yours. Let the Sun in your health and duties zone dictate what you should do for others and how you should look after your body.

Thursday 21st

Check in with your personal values now. The long-term plans that were set in place earlier this year may need to be revisited. Do they still hold importance for you? If they do, remember that to achieve success you must play by the rules and follow the steps.

Friday 22nd

Your mood may be much more stable today. This might be because you have found a way to please everyone without compromising yourself. You could be surprised at reactions from others which are not as negative as you think. Return to your personal goals and not the shared ones.

Saturday 23rd

Try not to be too fixed in your opinions today. You might notice that you're more inclined to speak out and try new ways of working, but not those suggested by others. You don't always know best and would benefit from the wisdom of others experience.

Sunday 24th

If you persist in being stubborn, nothing will get done and you will regret wasting a weekend. Things might blow up in your face if you don't toe the line and play nicely with others. You could find that your health suffers and you give yourself a stressful day. Is it worth it?

Monday 25th

Your mood could lift today and everyone around you will breathe a sigh of relief. A family member or person in authority could be responsible for making you see sense. Use empathy and duty combined to get results. Harmony can be achieved by evening and family harmony restored.

Tuesday 26th

Be cautious today. The planetary energy suggests the potential for outbursts. However, this energy can also be good for genius thinking and problem-solving. Work through your day as if it's a puzzle or quest to be solved and you can come out of it a winner without a fight involved.

Wednesday 27th

Your emotions are flavoured with harmony, truth, justice and dreams today. This can be a good thing as it means that you're back on track with your inner compass. You are facing your true north. Keep it in sight as the day progresses and watch for the effect this has.

Thursday 28th

Finding a practical workaround for a mundane problem could be easier than you think today. You must be methodical and put some physical energy behind your mental processes. You could be making something useful or learning how to use a new tool. This could be a money-making venture for you.

Friday 29th

Pluto turns retrograde today. Here begins another time where you reinvent your home surroundings. This might mean trying out a new look, a new job or some serious DIY. It's likely that you have done this often over the last few years, but you haven't found what you're looking for yet.

Saturday 30th

A new moon and solar eclipse open a window of wild card energy. This will almost certainly involve what you do for pleasure, finances and your day to day duties. There are also blessings to be accessed as your ruler, Jupiter, meets up with Venus who can bring harmony, beauty and abundance.

MAY

Sunday 1st

You could be prone to emotional outbursts today. Money may be involved which could also mean that you have a spending spree or make a large impulse buy. It may feel as if you have to do something immediately or the chance will be gone. Think carefully before indulging.

Monday 2nd

This morning you could be optimistic or dreamy. Either way, this is a good start to the week. Partners are highlighted and you may be having useful discussions which deepen your level of relating to each other. A romantic evening could appease your need for harmony between the two of you.

Tuesday 3rd

Keep an eye on your energy levels today. You might find that you're unable to stay focused and procrastinate greatly. You might simply need to disconnect from others and work alone. There may be too many distractions which don't help your concentration. Refrain from projecting your mood onto others.

Wednesday 4th

Vague feelings may flow into your awareness and leave you with an unsettling sense that something isn't right. However, this can also be a catalyst for you to make something happen. Family and daily duties seem to be the theme. Perhaps you've overlooked an important job or message.

Thursday 5th

Today the planetary energy is rather unstable. You might want to hide away or make plans to cook favourite foods and nurture yourself. It might be difficult to get time alone, so find a trusted friend or partner with whom you feel safe and protected. Physical exercise can also help.

Friday 6th

Loving discussions can be useful now. If you're worried about how a partner perceives you, talk to them. Your self-worth and urge to please can both be satisfied by connecting and being honest. Creative projects can also flourish if you put pen to paper and express yourself openly.

Saturday 7th

Much better energy can enable you to enjoy a weekend of fun and laughter. Put your physical energy into something you enjoy. This could be a DIY project or a day out in nature. Your emotions may entice you to make grand gestures. Ensure that you can back these up with action.

Sunday 8th

You could be full of inspiration and wish to do something creative or romantic. This is also a good time to plan a holiday or trip abroad. You may be thinking about travelling or taking up a course of study. Don't let your mundane duties prevent you from growing.

Monday 9th

The working week begins with a downturn in your mood. This might be because you feel restricted or have suddenly realised that you haven't done enough in the wider world. You may now have the urge to remedy this. Communicate or connect with people who can help make this a reality.

Tuesday 10th

Mercury turns retrograde today. This will happen in your relationship zone, so be mindful that your partnership could be strained. Do all the usual preparations and back up devices and check travel plans. Take extra care over the next few weeks not to cause unnecessary strife between you and a loved one.

Wednesday 11th

Jupiter jumps into your romance and creative zone today. As your ruler, he will bring blessings and abundance in this area now. Practical activity is best done today, but you may be resentful that there's no time to dream or play. You could be juggling family and work duties.

Thursday 12th

Your interest groups and friendships may feel the first negative effect of Mercury's retrograde today. There could be miscommunication or a split within them which can cause disharmony. You may need to choose a side or be the peacemaker. This is minor, so don't fret too much.

Friday 13th

You could be struggling with lovers and friends now. This may be a difficult situation where you have to let someone down. You may not have the heart to do this and the decision could be taken out of your hands. Watch out for jealousy or rivalry.

Saturday 14th

The right thing to do might be walking away and having time alone. You might like to retreat and process your thoughts rather than take any action or speak your mind. Drop into your private thoughts and contemplate recent events. You can do a lot of deep soul-searching today.

Sunday 15th

Something from your subconscious may resurface today and cause you some stress. This could be an old and outdated way of behaving. Your childhood conditioning and habits may need to be reviewed. Take a look at how you can transform and heal old wounds. Dare to dream tonight, but remember your limitations.

Monday 16th

A full moon and lunar eclipse close a period of unsettling and unusual energy. You may have learned a thing or two about your natural reactions to criticism. Put your best foot forward today and face any challenges with curiosity and a willingness to learn. Communicate your feelings clearly.

Tuesday 17th

Today you may feel more inclined to keep the peace and harmony. You could be using your leadership skills and marching into a new project with confidence. This is a good time for romance and expressing your feelings towards someone special. Be bold, brave and lead with your heart.

Wednesday 18th

You may be more driven to achieve your goals now. You might be putting plans into action and using up excess energy to align with your inner compass. This could, however, disrupt family life if you're selfish about it. Remember that long-term goals aren't achieved in a day and to slow down.

Thursday 19th

Physical and practical activities can bring you peace of mind. You could be changing something in your home and putting down new roots elsewhere. This may be a turbulent time but has positive results and is nothing to be concerned about. Change and shifts are happening. Don't try to stop them.

Friday 20th

The future beckons and you can see the road ahead. This can feel good and propels you to accept new things. Communication can be broad today but can also be unclear or give you too much to think about. New romantic or creative ideas may be unrealistic or too large.

Saturday 21st

Although you may plan a weekend of doing your own thing, this may not actualise, and you could feel resentful. You could be called upon to keep up your responsibilities elsewhere. Check in with your body and your health now. Look out for messages and symbols this evening.

Sunday 22nd

You would be wise to use today to do family things. Something tells you to put down your dreams and personal goals today as they will still be there later. You could struggle with this and there may be tension or misunderstandings.

Monday 23rd

Is there something you've overlooked recently? You could be playing catch up today as there is a sense of urgency within you. This may be a chore or duty which needs completing. You may be retracing your steps or taking a second look at a project which hasn't brought satisfaction.

Tuesday 24th

You could be tempted to make concrete plans which align with your core values today. However, Mercury is asking you to think around them and ensure that you're not being deceived or unrealistic. Don't do anything just yet as something may come to light which changes your perception.

Wednesday 25th

Mars joins Venus in your romance zone. This can mean that your important relationship gets more passionate and active. It can also be a time of high productivity including heated discussions, so be careful. You could get a revelation on what needs to change or be discarded for your plans to take root.

Thursday 26th

Network and connect with people who can help you today. You could find a teacher who has valuable words of advice for you. Listen to what they say and take on board any lessons they offer. It's time to stretch your personal boundaries without hurting yourself or others.

Friday 27th

You may wake with a different way of looking at things today. This may feel uncomfortable as it's new to you, but will force you to spread your wings a little more. This will be beneficial in the long run. Plan for some luxury or indulgences this weekend. Good food and company will suffice.

Saturday 28th

You may have an itch that needs scratching today. This could be anything from a need to do something different, break free or an ingenious idea to pursue. Venus encourages you to eat well, get healthy and detox anything bad from your diet. Do something nice for yourself.

Sunday 29th

Today your mind could be far off into the distant future. Your dreams may be huge, and you could exhaust yourself by going over the top in anything you do today. Passions can be hot, and a romantic time may be on the agenda. Don't overwhelm a partner with your enthusiasm.

Monday 30th

A new moon in your relationship zone gives you a chance to set intentions regarding what you want from love. You may choose to learn something new or reconnect with a lost love. Your mind can be full of enquiry now, so slim it down and choose one attainable goal.

Tuesday 31st

You may be thinking about your role in the collective today. What part do you play? Where do you fit in? Any conclusions you draw may not be in line with your personal values. This might be something to consider as the year progresses. Does the group hold you back?

JUNE

....

Wednesday 1st

There could be small challenges to face today. These will concern your feelings of security and have you wondering if your creative pursuits are worth the effort. Stick with it as this is a passing phase. Cling to the fact that you are a unique individual, and your self-expression is important.

Thursday 2nd

You may feel more uplifted today and get some inspiration from outside sources. Pay attention to your health and wellbeing. It may be that you do too much for others and are beginning to feel the strain. It's your turn to be nourished and protected. Do what feeds your soul.

Friday 3rd

Mercury turns direct today. Anything you've put off whilst the retrograde was on, can now be returned to, maybe with fresh eyes. You may have a better view of your inner compass and know what needs to be discarded. Find your courage to do this and broaden your mind.

Saturday 4th

Saturn turns retrograde today. His annual lessons might teach you something about your communication style and things you'd like to learn. Your role in your interest groups may also be up for review. You could struggle with boundaries at this time. Know that they are there for a reason.

Sunday 5th

You might feel an urge to break free today. This could come from a need to explore or travel the world more. If you get an idea in your head now there may be no stopping you. Try researching areas of interest before committing to something.

Monday 6th

A fixed view or opinion may not help you much today. You are used to going with the flow and being adaptable, but today you could come across as stubborn and wilful. Put your mind to practical things and be methodical in your thinking. You could win points by being diligent at work.

Tuesday 7th

Earthy energy may conflict with your need to be fiery and passionate. This may be telling you that your best work is done when you're more grounded and concentrating on the job in hand. Use up your excess physical energy with exercise or connecting with nature.

Wednesday 8th

Your dreams may seem too far away today. Alternatively, you may be tired and drained. Manage this by getting on with your daily chores and once they're done, take time to recharge your batteries. Friends and social groups can help you lift your mood and balance your emotions.

Thursday 9th

Today there may be a conflict between your wider circle of friends and your personal hobbies. It may be that you feel some guilt about spending time with groups and not paying enough attention to your own things. This will pass, so enjoy your social life for the time being.

Friday 10th

Your mental abilities can be overwhelmed today. Perhaps you've been problem-solving and have come up against a brick wall. Leave it alone for now and come back to it later. You could be enjoying quiet time this evening to process your thoughts and come up with a solution by yourself.

Saturday 11th

Plan to do something out of the ordinary this weekend. A little self-care might surprise you and lift your spirits. Luxuries and simple pleasures will please you. You might also surprise someone else by doing something nice for them. Entertaining at home could be a good way to offer your services to another.

Sunday 12th

Something from the past creeps to the surface and stares you in the face. This might be a healing opportunity and one which may involve looking at your relationship with finances and shared investments. You could be idealistic now, so keep it real.

Monday 13th

The Moon drops into your sign and you feel more like yourself. You can be more outgoing and optimistic now. The wider world is waiting for you to explore and you should make some plans for summer travel. Mercury re-enters your relationship zone. Discuss the possibility of a holiday with a loved one.

Tuesday 14th

A full moon in your own sign can put you in the spotlight. What have you achieved in the last six months? What might have come to fruition for you now? You may feel that it isn't much, but look closer, this is an opportunity to push yourself a little further.

Wednesday 15th

Remember that the key to success is to follow the rules
and not to miss out any steps. You may feel restricted today
because you want to run before you can walk. Try to round
yourself with practical work and appreciate that not everything
needs to be a quick fix.

Thursday 16th

You could feel as if you will implode today. There is push and
pull energy out there which can be enticing yet confining. If
you can change just one thing today, make it something that
can clear up space for you to achieve your dreams.

Friday 17th

Today you may be calmer and accept that you need to put
in the work to get where you want to go. You could be drawn
back to your creative or romantic adventures. A new or
fresh look at an old project can breathe life into it once
more. Use this energy well.

Saturday 18th

If you wish to start a revolution, make it a small one which is
over by teatime. You may be rebellious and want to spend the
day doing something wild. You know that this might not be a
good idea, so settle for connecting with loved ones and your
unique friendships.

Sunday 19th

A family day might be the thing to settle your restless energy
today. You might get a positive boost simply by being amongst
your tribe, going with the flow and merging with the general
feel of family. Share your dreams with others and they will
likely support and encourage you.

Monday 20th

Your inner compass asks you to connect and realign if need be. You could be pleasantly surprised with how in sync you actually are. There could be something outstanding regarding your one-to-one relationships. This may be something that was left unsaid or a decision which has now been made.

Tuesday 21st

The summer solstice occurs today and is a time of pause. You may like to consider how far you've come this year so far. The longest day brings blessings and you may like to share these with your partner or close friend. You could even find a muse today.

Wednesday 22nd

Your energy and emotions are intermingled today, and you may find that you're exhausted or exhilarated. Whichever it is, it will certainly involve romance or creativity and can be filled with expression. You can be more passionate and driven and there could be fireworks. However, beware of burnout.

Thursday 23rd

Venus enters your relationship zone now. You could be more inclined to sweet romance or maintaining the harmony in your partnerships. Venus also attracts money, so there could be something you spend on as a couple or you unite your minds for a deeper level of understanding.

Friday 24th

Today is another explosive day with potentially mind-blowing or draining energy. You will need to ensure that your mundane chores are all done before the weekend kicks off. You could be emotionally unstable and need to let off some steam with people you trust. You may be given a welcome surprise.

Saturday 25th

You will need to remember that you have responsibilities to others today. This could include simply acknowledging their rights and maintaining healthy boundaries between you. You can set about switching things up at home or with your bank balance now. This can help you on your personal journey and can make you feel good.

Sunday 26th

Today, romance is favoured, and you might spend the day with your lover or by being good to yourself. Your ruler, Jupiter, is offering blessings and asks that you stay curious and follow any line of enquiry which might help you connect and relate on a deeper level.

Monday 27th

Your head and heart are in sync. There may be many avenues you wish to explore with a loved one now. However, keep it healthy and be mindful of personal boundaries. If you overstep the mark you could undo everything you've built up so far this year. Respect your partner's wishes.

Tuesday 28th

Neptune turns retrograde today. As your inner compass, you might find that you have less clarity on your dreams and visions. Use this time to assess if what you want still holds value for you. It can be a confusing time, so go easy on yourself if you make mistakes.

Wednesday 29th

A new moon is a green light period to start something new. This might be a deeper connection to your soul's needs. You can be more introspective now and go to places within you that have previously frightened you. Use your intuition and look for what nourishes and nurtures you.

Thursday 30th

You could feel vulnerable today. It may be that someone is doing their best to care for you and it now feels a little smothering. Try not to react harshly as this is well-meant and your childhood habits and defence mechanisms are instinctively kicking in. They're outdated and unhelpful now.

JULY
· · · · · · · · · · · · · · · · · ·

Friday 1st
Be brave and go after what you desire today. You could be lucky in love today and have time to enjoy romance and luxury this evening. Speak from the heart and you could be rewarded with simple pleasures which mean a lot. Remember, little acts of kindness work both ways.

Saturday 2nd
Weekend chores can take up some of your time today and challenge you to think outside the box. You may be too stubborn or fixed in your views to accept something different. An urge to travel or get away might bring resentment or yearning. Think of alternative ways to satisfy this.

Sunday 3rd
If you're bold enough to speak your mind, be sure you can back it up with honest action. Discussions with a loved one may be enlightening and encouraging. Change your focus from what you feel is beyond your capabilities to what you can easily achieve. A realistic approach will work.

Monday 4th
You may have deadlines to meet and could be rushing to get something finished this week. This could also be something you need to get off your chest before it's too late. Use your intuition and check every detail before committing to something even if it means denying yourself a treat.

Tuesday 5th

As two planets change signs, you might sense your mental and physical energy shift. You could be thinking more deeply and applying your drive to rooting down and fixing something in solid ground. This could be tiring as it might be an unexpected change in your usual routine.

Wednesday 6th

Other people might demand your attention today and you may have to let them down or politely decline a social invitation. Your own needs take precedence now. Little disturbances may seem larger than they are, but this mood will pass over. Stick to your guns and do your own thing.

Thursday 7th

You have a good chance to balance social groups with what you need from one-to-one relationships. You might find an ally who becomes your confidante or partner in crime. You may also find a teacher who can show you the art of subtle communication.

Friday 8th

Self-reflection would be a good activity now. You could feel challenged to be present for others but may need time alone to filter and transmute your thoughts and feelings. Introspection can be helpful now and may offer a different perspective for you to consider. Go as deeply as you dare.

Saturday 9th

You can be more emotional now but might be keeping it under wraps. This is fine unless there is something you need to share with another. You could feel slightly restless as material from your psyche shifts and asks to be dealt with. Release your worries one at a time.

Sunday 10th

A sleepless night may have given you the answers you seek. These might concern making changes or dealing with old problems that still bother you. The Moon in your sign gives you cause to be active and get out into the world. Physical exercise would be good for you today.

Monday 11th

Be cautious today as you could be leading up to a selfish night which won't go down too well with others. If you feel that your needs aren't being met by a partner, spend your time on your creative projects. You could be working through the night to get something finished.

Tuesday 12th

Hard work and dedication will fuel you through the day. You must put your personal goals aside for now. However, if you're free to work on them and all your obligations have been met, you could have great success by applying the same energy to them, just don't overdo it.

Wednesday 13th

Today's full moon can show you what has manifested for you regarding your status, home and values. Are you seeing more quality in your immediate surroundings now? If this hasn't come to much, you have a chance to look at what didn't work and make adjustments for the future.

Thursday 14th

You could be grieving a loss or something which didn't work out as expected. It might be time to honestly evaluate its part in your life and accept that it may not have been meant for you. Talking to like-minded folk can boost your confidence and make you feel better.

Friday 15th

You could be filled with restless energy today and at the same time, you might feel stuck. This is a good time to pause and assess the situation before taking a leap of faith. There may be a wise teacher who can offer you alternative routes to consider. Know your limits today.

Saturday 16th

Be good to yourself now. You might turn to your family of origin for support and nourishment. Going back to your roots and exploring the hidden depths might trigger a few old feelings. Go with where they take you as you could find the treasure you buried long ago.

Sunday 17th

You might be extra emotional today, so again, go easy and don't beat yourself up for perceived failures. You could experience a surprise or two. These might come in the form of words of love spoken honestly and unexpectedly. Take them as they're meant, with genuine feelings. Respond respectfully and be honest.

. . . .

Monday 18th

Your inner compass is in sight and you could come back to alignment with fresh eyes and new hope. However, you may still be disillusioned, so tread carefully. There's no need to give the whole of yourself up for examination now, just be humble and accept any support you're given.

Tuesday 19th

Although your feelings are huge, you may have more need for truth and fair play. It's likely that your intuition is trying to tell you something important today. Make sure you listen. It's time to step into your truth and walk your talk. Your words count; make sure they're heard.

Wednesday 20th

All the changes and shifts that have happened recently are exposed today. This can be overwhelming but is also necessary for you to track your route forward. Think of this as phase two of this year's growth. The groundwork has been done and now the hard work begins.

Thursday 21st

This may be a draining day, so be careful with your energy. You might be too emotionally attached to a duty or obligation. You may also be determined to finish a job and put everything you've got into it. Pay attention to your intuition today as you could receive some information.

Friday 22nd

The energy today is unstable, and you may still be suffering from burnout. Find a way of using that excess energy in a way which doesn't hurt anyone, including yourself. A lesson is presented to you now and you would do well to remember your personal boundaries.

Saturday 23rd

Take a day off and spend some quality time with a partner or person you admire. You could have a lot to process and another mind can help filter out the rubbish you don't need. Making plans for travel or going somewhere for the day could bring satisfaction.

Sunday 24th

You may have a mind filled with possibilities and wish to act on these. These may include romantic adventures or simply something nice that you and a lover could enjoy together. Your creativity is high, and you may think of an activity which involves other cultures, philosophies and religions. Higher learning may also attract you.

Monday 25th

You could experience a conflict today between wanting to go within and take care of your deepest needs and enjoying time with a partner. You may be reassessing your dreams and visions and looking through any illusions you've been under. Take time for self-nurturing this evening.

Tuesday 26th

A tricky day means that you need to feel safe and protected. You must plan for self-care this evening. This can mean cooking your favourite foods and hiding out under your duvet. Make yourself unavailable to others and switch off. Look after yourself now and preserve your personal energy.

Wednesday 27th

As your mood lifts, you find that you're willing to oblige people who need your help. Your mundane duties can be done with ease and leave you time for contemplation this evening. Realign with your inner compass to feel balanced and whole again. Use your energy on things you enjoy doing.

Thursday 28th

A new moon arrives and is the perfect opportunity to set intentions to travel, study or seek the truth of life's mysteries. Set yourself a goal to expand your horizons in some way. However, your ruler, Jupiter, turns retrograde and might get you to slow down and rethink any existing plans.

Friday 29th

Today can bring challenges of all sorts. You could be irritable and impatient this evening. This may be because you have sensed Jupiter's lesson for you this year and the slower pace doesn't suit you. Use this time to make all of your plans as watertight as you can.

Saturday 30th

Your head and heart are in sync now. Restrictions may be placed on your communications and learning, but you recognise the need to curb your impulses. As frustrating as this is, you will soon adapt and reap the benefits. Be sure-footed and take one step at a time.

Sunday 31st

Be careful what you say today. Your mouth could run away with and you run the risk of upsetting an elder or person in authority. The way forward may require you to step into the unknown or look at a new skill you need to master. This can be both exciting and daunting.

AUGUST

·················

Monday 1st

An auspicious day with high energy could propel you into a
future path. Part of this might involve how you care for others
and what you do daily to tick along. Changes are ahead and
you may not be able to refuse. Go along for the ride and see
what you can learn.

Tuesday 2nd

You may get a glimpse of how you can prepare and look after
your own needs whilst all around you seems like turmoil.
This could be the moment you realise that your own safety
is paramount. Finding a home and work balance is more
important now.

Wednesday 3rd

Your desires and drive could be working alongside each other
to achieve results. You might feel this and have some doubts,
but if you play by the rules and give it a chance, you can
succeed in protecting yourself whilst attending to your duties
and obligations. Be noticeably clear in your communications.

Thursday 4th

Your mind is ready to shift its focus now. You could be more
willing to research and unearth every tiny detail before making
a commitment or forging ahead with your work. An analytical
approach to your work can give you reassurance and more self-
worth. Be a detective and scrutinise everything.

Friday 5th

An introspective mood may have you reflecting on past actions or circumstances. You could get extra moody and negative now. Try not to blow things out of proportion until you've thought it all through. Something from your deepest psyche, a grudge perhaps, needs to go before you can move on.

Saturday 6th

Your emotions may be close to the surface today. You may be thinking deeply and darkly which can cause negative thoughts and self-talk. Focus on your own basic needs and remember that you are worthy of good things. An evening out or doing what you enjoy may be good for you.

Sunday 7th

Whilst you may be unable to fix your train of thoughts today, you are able to consider your personal goals. You might even notice that they've shifted slightly as you could be changing your perspective and making adjustments. Let your natural energy inspire you to march onwards.

Monday 8th

Today you must concentrate on what you need to learn to get ahead. This may involve researching around a new topic or acknowledging that some things aren't meant for you. You may not have a choice about this. Be sensible and accept the rules or traditions you feel bound by.

Tuesday 9th

You could sense subtle manipulation or passive aggression around you now. This can indicate what you need to feel safe and nurtured. If you must let something go, perhaps a project which has been weighing you down, do so with kindness. Be practical and you will see the sense in this.

Wednesday 10th

This is an important day where you could see your energy spurred on by external influences. You can achieve a great deal today if you stick to the job in hand. You may see the necessity of ending something which no longer serves you. As hard as it is, you will benefit ultimately.

Thursday 11th

If you've assessed your personal needs and understand your own limits, now is the time to express these. Venus can help you go after what you want. You can expect more quality and maybe a boost in finances. All you need to do is speak your truth.

Friday 12th

A full moon can highlight how your learning, teaching and communication have progressed this year. You may find yourself closer to your community or taking a leadership role. A new responsibility may mean that you must shift your focus to the needs of the wider groups you're involved with.

Saturday 13th

Your family may require your attention this weekend, so try to be available. However, you could also be taking work home with you which can present a struggle to balance everyone's needs. Don't work too hard. Schedule time for relaxation and connection with your loved ones. Remember that your roots support your shoots.

Sunday 14th

Nice energy can help you to merge with your tribe and focus on your inner compass. You may be doing home improvements or making your environment more appealing. Although you still might wish to get away or have a break, you can stick to your responsibilities and plan later.

Monday 15th

You could be yearning for a holiday now but feel that you have too much to do at home. Your romantic relationship will benefit if you make plans for a short trip. It doesn't have to be exotic; it can be closer to home and still feed your sense of adventure.

Tuesday 16th

You may be more optimistic today as you say what's on your mind and it feels good. Others may be surprised at your confidence and determination to do something unusual or risky. Don't let others dissuade you from trying something new and out of your comfort zone.

Wednesday 17th

Today you must root down and simply get on with your mundane duties. It might be a good idea to check in with your health and pay attention to any niggles you may have been having. Stop ignoring signs of ill health, however small they are. Check that your body has all it needs.

Thursday 18th

Be mindful today because the energy suggests that you could be impulsive and volatile. You might be stubbornly rebelling against limitations. A sense of urgency will need to be carefully assessed as this could be detrimental to your wellbeing. Physical exercise can get rid of excess energy.

Friday 19th

Determination might be your downfall today. If you persist in going against the grain and seeking short-term pleasures, you could find that it backfires on you. Ground your energy and do activities which bring in results that last. Your duties and responsibilities must come before any wild ideas.

Saturday 20th

It may be tricky to rein yourself in today. Turn to a partner for support and they may give you an alternative viewpoint to consider. You could have a dialogue with your inner voice and thrash through a few ideas you've been having recently.

Sunday 21st

Too much flexible thinking can get you into a muddle today. You might need to distract yourself until you have more clarity. A partner or person you admire can give you a more balanced idea of what needs to be done to feel successful and in line with your true self.

Monday 22nd

Shine brightly today. You could be using your innate talents to get what you need. This can be in your romance or your creative projects. Use your intuition to expand your thinking. Look deep within you and you could find a solution to recent concerns. This might mean ending something.

Tuesday 23rd

Now is the time to settle into a new routine and look at what you can offer to others. You may find that you can be of service in ways which also declutter your own life from negative baggage. Deep introspection and a thorough check-in with your personal needs are required.

Wednesday 24th

Uranus turns retrograde today. This might feel like a shift in your mundane duties and a shake-up of your routine. Embrace this change as it comes with new opportunities for you to explore. You might feel exposed and uncomfortable, but you will soon adapt to your new circumstances.

Thursday 25th

If something is outstanding or you have a deadline to meet, act on it now. You might need to knuckle down and do what is asked of you and ignore your own needs today. However, this will go a long way and can help you in the workplace or higher education.

Friday 26th

Today you are more in touch with your desires and they may simply be that you wish to connect with friends more. Plan for some fun and relaxation with your social groups this weekend. An underlying feeling of irritability might hinder your mood. Be mindful when communicating with elders.

Saturday 27th

A new moon can be a good time to set your goals and intentions regarding work, career and what you need to declutter from your life. You may also be starting something which you have anxiety about. Perhaps you have second thoughts or doubts about your ability to succeed.

Sunday 28th

Shifts are happening and you may be having concerns. You must take a leap of faith and trust that the unease you're feeling is helping you grow. Accept the challenge and use your natural ability to explore new ground, to conquer your fears. All will be well when you've come to terms with it.

Monday 29th

You might have to call upon your interest groups for support and encouragement. You could need your tribe now. Your mind can be soothed if you spend time with like-minded friends and associates who can offer words of wisdom. Take on board any advice you're given and mull it over in your private time.

Tuesday 30th

You must put your creative projects on hold, but know that they will always be there for you to come back to. For now, your energy must be put into assimilating new ways of working. By evening you might have more of an idea of how to advance.

Wednesday 31st

An emotional attachment to something might mean that you have a hard time adjusting today. However, take time off and go easy on yourself. Honour what this once meant to you and know that you've made space for more valuable and useful things to come into your life.

SEPTEMBER

Thursday 1st

Leaving a piece of your past behind could bring up some unwanted or hurtful memories. This is the best time to look at what needs healing. It could be that your instinctual responses which once kept you safe, no longer serve you. A more mature approach is needed.

Friday 2nd

Your inner world continues to shake as you may be projecting your unwanted baggage elsewhere. Notice if you're clashing with people and why this is. Fix on just one of your personal dreams today and take steps towards it. Growth is always preceded by discomfort.

Saturday 3rd

The Moon lands in your sign today but could reinforce negative feelings, particularly within your relationships. Watch for any signs of selfishness and refrain from projecting these onto people you care about. Words can hurt, so try not to use them carelessly. Think of how you can best fit in with the collective.

Sunday 4th

You have a chance to stand up, be bold and say what's on your mind today. It's better that people know how you feel rather than to keep it all inside. You could realise that not everyone is out to get you and your support team can be found within your family of origin.

Monday 5th

Stick to the daily routine today and put your mind to your tasks. You could be itching to begin something new but don't have all the necessary details yet. You would be unwise to jump the gun and work alone. Venus in your career sign can boost your confidence.

Tuesday 6th

Make the most of the grounding energy today. You might have more of an understanding of the route ahead and can plan careful and practical steps towards achieving your goals. Your inner compass is in sight and you may feel the shift is more comfortable now.

Wednesday 7th

Clarity comes when you are more settled. Ask others for help if you need it. There's no point struggling alone because of your pride. You will find that your productivity is higher, and this means that you've adjusted, maybe in part, to your new vision and goals. Let ideas flow through you.

Thursday 8th

Don't return to a fixed way of thinking just yet. There may be a need to learn more about a new topic or get involved with your wider community. Allow yourself to be open to other views or you risk clashing with those who could be your most valuable assets now.

Friday 9th

You could be tired and winding down ready for the weekend. As long as you get all your work done, you can plan to spend time doing things you love. Family members may be a hindrance but also show that they're there for you when you need them.

Saturday 10th

Mercury turns retrograde today in your friends zone.
You will need to review group ventures now. Back up all
devices and double-check travel plans. Be extra careful when
communicating or dealing with your social connections.
A full moon can spotlight family issues, compassion and
empathy. Time spent with parents can be moving today.

Sunday 11th

You might want to get back to a creative project which you
started but put to one side. A break may have let you look at
it differently and you may now approach it with fresh energy.
This is also true for romantic relationships where you must
tread carefully.

Monday 12th

Today you feel as if you've got your groove back and can
make forward progress with a partner who is on the same
wavelength as you. The energy is easy-going, and you might
receive words of wisdom from an elder in the community.
Don't rock the boat by being radical.

Tuesday 13th

You can say goodbye to something which has had a negative
impact on you recently. This might make you resentful of the
time and energy you've spent on it. Settle down into your daily
routine and be productive as this will always raise your spirits
and self-worth.

Wednesday 14th

Grounding energy can mean that you adapt to your work easily today. It can also give you cause for excitement as you feel something bubbling under the surface. You could reward yourself this evening with a favourite meal or a workout to make your body feel nourished and pleasured.

Thursday 15th

Continue doing practical or physical things which uplift you. You might now see that you don't need to go at full speed all the time. This is what your ruler, Jupiter, has been teaching you. Partner time this evening can be pleasant, however, you may also be exhausted and prefer to be alone.

Friday 16th

Tread carefully today. There is some unsettled energy around which means that you could clash with others. Remember that Mercury in retrograde asks that you take time to consider your responses and aim for clarity. Opposite points of view may cause a problem this evening and drain your energy.

Saturday 17th

You will need to be mindful of your behaviour today. You could be close to an emotional outburst which can upset others and put you in the doghouse. You would be better off taking time off and lying low until this mood of yours passes. You may not be good company today.

Sunday 18th

Recent energy can touch on your safety needs. You should retreat into your shell today and do things which feed your soul. There is too much going on for you to process, so you may simply need to look after yourself or sleep on it. Nothing will get done today.

Monday 19th

You could have a better idea of what you need to feel good now. This may be home comforts, or it may be time alone to declutter and organise your innermost thoughts. More stirrings from your psyche can be unsettling but act as a warning sign. Are you still out of sync?

Tuesday 20th

Conflicting energy can mean that you waver between emotional and practical thinking. You may be feeling vulnerable and exposed. Wait until evening when you are surer of yourself and find your voice again. Have the courage to step out of your comfort zone.

Wednesday 21st

You might wish to review your creative projects today. It may be possible to see where you've been following a path not meant for you. You might also notice that your grand ideas aren't always achievable and slimming them down to manageable sizes would be better. Give yourself credit for the idea in the first place.

115

Thursday 22nd

Deadlines at work may need your attention. See to it that nothing gets in the way of your priorities now. Daydreaming or trying to do things differently can be a waste of time. Stick to the tried and tested way of approaching problems as being inventive could raise further delays.

Friday 23rd

You may be returning to a problem or issue within your wider social groups now. Do what you can by listening to all sides and weighing up where you fit in. It may be best for you to retreat altogether if this doesn't feel right to you.

Saturday 24th

You could struggle with work and family time now. It could be that your duties in your career have taken you away from obligations within the family. A balancing act is needed and if you can't manage this, learn to say no to extra chores which take up your valuable free time.

Sunday 25th

As tiredness persists, you may feel that some areas of your life are draining you. This would be a good time to review this as a new moon suggests a new start and a chance to balance things you do for others with activities you enjoy for yourself.

Monday 26th

Give your inner voice a chance to talk today. You may find that you've been neglecting yourself recently. Ask yourself what you can change to make yourself more open and freer to be the person you want to be. Spend time thinking about recreating your personal world and its boundaries.

Tuesday 27th

Your mental faculties could be working overtime now, so make sure that it's worth it. You could try doing something practical and methodical in order to ground your ideas and ensure that they will work for you. This might mean a complete change of your views on what adds quality to your life.

Wednesday 28th

Find the place within you where you can dialogue with your inner voice. You may need to check in and see if you're being totally honest with yourself. Bravado may be your default when making tough decisions, but they may not always be the right ones for you.

Thursday 29th

Those familiar rumblings in your psyche are back to remind you that growth doesn't happen without some measure of discomfort. You may need to learn to rely on others more or to accept your own limits. You can stretch these gently, but breaking through them roughly no longer helps you.

Friday 30th

The Moon returns to your sign and you can stand tall knowing that you're prepared to look at yourself objectively now. At least, for the time being, you could have a better sense of your personal boundaries and what drains your energy. Reserve judgements and refrain from being impulsive.

OCTOBER
. . . .

Saturday 1st
Catching up with friends and relatives could be a good thing
to do today as you may not in the right space to pay attention
to much else. Your presence may be needed by an elder or a
person in authority. Don't try to force anything which isn't
coming naturally today.

Sunday 2nd
Mercury turns direct today and you could find yourself going
over old ground once again. This may be an opportunity to
check on details you may have missed during and before
retrograde. However, this could be tiresome and leave you
feeling like you've had an unproductive weekend.

Monday 3rd
Social contacts could be at odds with you which means that
you need to find a workable solution to a problem. This could
play on your mind today until you or the group are ready to
accept something new. This will all work out fine if you group
together to find an innovative solution.

Tuesday 4th
Communications which are open and honest can put some
new energy into existing projects. You could find a teacher
who can inspire you to work within the boundaries that you
have. Friends and interest groups can also be supportive
and offer quality ideas which could be moneymaking and
raise your self-esteem.

Wednesday 5th

Today you may notice that group efforts can make things easier than forging ahead by yourself. Once you've found the answer to a problem, fix it in your mind. You could find that you're getting emotionally attached to doing things by the book now and this boosts your confidence.

Thursday 6th

Watery energy aids you in going with the flow of the collective. Family members can be a part of this. If you find yourself more inclined to be compassionate and patient with others, you can be rewarded with free-flowing unconditional love. Let yourself drift with this nice energy.

Friday 7th

The little voice in your head reminds you that making permanent changes or endings makes space for new growth. You may now see a wide-open space in front of you. Don't be in a rush to fill it. Take time to consider the best way forward.

Saturday 8th

Your inner compass is in sight and you may be amazed at how much it has shifted this year. It might be hard to believe that slowing down and looking at things from different angles has given you a more responsible approach to achieving your potential. This bodes well for your creative projects.

Sunday 9th

Pluto turns direct now, and you could be looking at how much your value system has changed. What you've thrown to the cosmic waste bin this year is testament to your growth and maturity. A full moon showcases how far you've come in your creative and romantic pursuits.

. . . .

Monday 10th

There may be another deadline to meet today. This could simply be putting the finishing touches to a work project or finalising a deal you stepped back from recently. You may now see the benefit of holding back until the time is right to act. Get ready to rededicate yourself to your goals.

Tuesday 11th

Your social life may get lively now as Mercury re-enters this area and needs you to have some fun and laughter. You can return to thinking about the simple pleasures you enjoy and how you give your time to others. Schedule some activities with your best friends now.

Wednesday 12th

You may be presented with minor challenges today which can be overcome by thinking outside the box. Put your inventive side into action, but remember to keep it real, remember your limitations and abide by the rules. Another mountain to conquer might appeal to your sense of adventure.

Thursday 13th

Mental energy can set your mind racing and scheming again. Put this to good use and plan events for the upcoming festive season. Your friends and partner will thank you for your inspiration and clever ideas. Let your partner have their say today and between you, a grand plan may emerge.

Friday 14th

You may be stepping up and leading the way today. However, if young people are looking up to you, be sure to be responsible and respectful. You may be hosting a get-together with like-minded folk and this can boost your ego. Stay modest and allow others an opinion.

Saturday 15th

Your mental energy is high now, but is also at risk of being draining for others. Make sure that you don't get carried away with the sound of your own voice. You might need to tame it down a little. Gather your resources and enjoy a night of comfort, security and nurturing.

Sunday 16th

Take a day of rest. You could be more tired than you think. Do something which can help you recharge your batteries. Try cooking your favourite foods, enjoying good company or deepening your interests with reading around topics which fascinate you. Feed your soul and you will be refreshed for the week ahead.

Monday 17th

The week begins with some challenging aspects from your mundane duties. Don't push too hard to rectify these, a solution will present itself if you listen to your intuition. If you feel vulnerable, understand that you may have exerted your mental processes too much and need more rest time.

Tuesday 18th

You can be more outgoing now and have reset your natural default button which is filled with energy. You may have wiped the slate clean with a romance or creative idea and can pause before you decide what to do next. Don't repeat any mistakes you've made recently.

Wednesday 19th

Stubbornness won't get you far today, but you might still try to push your opinions onto others. If your energy comes across as stroppy or childish, you may lose what you've gained, and this could knock your confidence again. Retreat and wait until this mood passes. Be humble and accept when you're in the wrong.

Thursday 20th

Better energy brings you back to yourself and you might find that you can see more clearly. Your energy and drive have more compassion and what you desire now is harmony. From where you're standing – a place of passion and inspiration – draw upon others for their logic and reasoning.

Friday 21st

A quiet day can give you space to work on your tasks without interruption or distraction. Be methodical and practical tasks can be easily mastered. You may have a way of helping others in the workplace which is valued. Be mindful of this today as respect will come your way.

Saturday 22nd

A last-minute invitation can come as a pleasant surprise. Snap it up or you could regret it. You may think it's not your thing and won't enjoy it, but try it. It could be the very thing which releases some pressure and lightens your load.

Sunday 23rd

Saturn turns direct now. What have you learned about boundaries, communication and authority figures this year? You will have time to contemplate and play around in your psyche now as Venus and the Sun drop into your most private thoughts. Self-care and healing will be the themes for the coming month, so pay attention.

Monday 24th

Your wider groups and social contacts ask for your attention now. It could be that plans are being made and they need you involved. As your mind and heart are in sync, you could accept anything that comes along as pleasant chatter and light-hearted interactions appeal to you.

Tuesday 25th

A new moon and solar eclipse throw open a window of time for you to dig around in your psyche and look at what old habits and conditioning need to be healed. This will be easier than you think. Revelations can be catalysts for inner change which will lead to a more mature you.

Wednesday 26th

You could feel some discomfort today, but remember that this is the irritation that provokes change and growth and is not to be feared. Don't make a return to your old way of thinking about authority today because it will undo all the good work you've done this year.

Thursday 27th

Listen to your dreams today as you may get some insight about partners or friendships. This could also be an event which can involve everyone you care for. You might be willing to go the extra mile for others today as your mood is optimistic.

Friday 28th

Jupiter retrogrades back into your family zone and suggests that there's something you need to return to there. An extra boost of compassion and empathy may be needed in dealing with some members of your tribe. If you manage this responsibly you will be admired and thanked.

Saturday 29th

Mercury joins the other planets in your private zone now. This can feel like fast progress is being made when looking for the gold you hide from others. What talents do you dumb down or have long forgotten about? Can they be resurrected now? Don't be afraid to showcase them.

Sunday 30th

Mars turns retrograde in your partner zone. This can slow things right down but can also settle disputes or anything you've been questioning regarding your relationships. This might feel like stalemate energy where no progress is made, but you can also think about it as a pause and a time for review.

Monday 31st

It may already feel as if an ending is upon you. However, with endings come new beginnings so change your mindset and see if it feels different. This may also be a quickly passing mood, so don't change anything yet. Simply sit with your thoughts and emotions today.

NOVEMBER
· · · · · · · · · · · · · · · · · ·

Tuesday 1st

You might feel like the odds are stacked against you today. The
niggles and disturbances in your psyche may feel too raw for
you to deal with. Your role in your community asks a lot from
you and you may not be in the right frame of mind to oblige.

Wednesday 2nd

Be gentle with yourself and your partner. You could feel the
first effect of Mars retrograde this morning. Perhaps this will
be a misunderstanding. There may be a revelation this evening
where you come to terms with an old love issue. Let it go now
and move on.

Thursday 3rd

Smoother energy can make you deeply thoughtful and
introspective. You may be coming to terms with what needs
to be healed and feel far more comfortable about this process.
Good memories surface alongside poor ones to remind you
that not all of the past was a waste of time and effort.

Friday 4th

Look at your inner compass now. You could see that although
it's shifted, you are still heading in the right direction. Little
or no action in your relationship sector is nothing to be
concerned about. Remember that this is a time to pause and
review things. Positive change requires a lot of patience.

Saturday 5th

You might have started a low fire burning which is now needing your attention. This could be that you're going back to the roots of your romance or a passion for art. You could receive more insight into what you need to remove from your life.

Sunday 6th

Do the right thing and act responsibly today. You can benefit by considering personal boundaries. A light bulb turns on in your hidden parts and suddenly makes everything clear. You might wonder why you've never thought of it before. Gossip or half-truths could make more sense now. Listen to your intuition.

Monday 7th

Do your daily duties and keep your head down today. You may wish to lie low and not have to think about your personal growth now. A tricky conversation could mean that you learn something distasteful. Take time to process what this means for you, but don't let it set you back.

Tuesday 8th

A full moon and lunar eclipse can close a window of wild card energy. This could reflect on your health and the things you value. Be on the alert for any subtle messages or signs from your deepest psyche as these can be signposts and show you the way through.

Wednesday 9th

You may feel like rebelling or breaking free from the daily grind, but think twice. This could be a knee-jerk reaction to something you've recently discovered. You could be more aware of events in the past that you have wrongly understood and carried with you as heavy baggage.

Thursday 10th

You might need to have difficult discussions with people, and this may be upsetting. However, this is a chance to put some puzzle pieces together and gain clarity over issues which have been rather fuzzy of late. In your heart, you may know that you've been disillusioned or kept away from the truth.

Friday 11th

Don't be too hard on yourself for not knowing something that you do now. This is a strange concept to get to grips with, but you mustn't reprimand your younger self. Be mindful that you don't project this onto a partner. They can support you if you share respectfully.

Saturday 12th

Step into your comfort zone and accept nurturing from others. You could be feeling exposed and vulnerable now and need extra care. The little voice in your head is still busy separating truth from deception and you may still be fragile. The dust is still settling on what you once believed.

Sunday 13th

Deep emotions may continue to swamp you. Let them flow around you, but make sure you have an anchor and fix yourself to land. Think of this an alchemical process which needs to occur. You could find that the unnecessary slips away and you're left with more clarity.

Monday 14th

You could be taking back control now and feel better about recent revelations. Your mood lifts and you could be more optimistic. You may even be brave enough to stand up and speak your truth. However, don't be brash or pushy. Show others that this has made you strong.

Tuesday 15th

It's possible that you could be more stubborn or refuse to be adaptable today. Others will just have to deal with it. You may be putting your foot down and making a bold statement. Just be careful as you don't want to cause more ripples. You need to be calm but firm.

Wednesday 16th

Venus enters your sign today. Your personal strength can be tempered with self-love and you could be presenting yourself as strong and passionate. Don't stand for any nonsense or let people push you around. You may have seen through someone who has been duping you all along.

Thursday 17th

Put your mind to different things today. Your methods of working and keen eye for detail can help you get through your working day. Mercury also enters your sign and your logical and rational brain will show others that you can be a force to be reckoned with. Attend to your duties to feel normal again.

Friday 18th

Spend the day on your mundane chores and get your 'to do' list ticked off. Practical chores can help you return to a sense of calm. By evening you may be tired and emotional but could have the time to relax and switch off. Do something quiet tonight.

Saturday 19th

You could be in the right mood to grab your friends and organise a social event. In fact, it could be you who makes the plans. Get all your weekend chores out of the way then let your hair down. It will do you good to let off some steam.

Sunday 20th

Catch up with people you may have neglected recently. A day of light-hearted chatter and connection might be the remedy you need to forget about upset and move on. You could find that an elder in the family is your best ally now and will know how to make you laugh.

Monday 21st

You could wake with a renewed sense of purpose and wish to continue with the things that bring you joy. These could be your romance or creative pursuits. There might be one last thing you need to clean up in the depths of your psyche.

Tuesday 22nd

The Sun enters your sign today. This is your birthday month. Happy Birthday! If you're still having an emotional attachment to recent revelations, do something practical or physical to get it out of your system. You should be able to shake this off if it surfaces again. It's no longer important.

Wednesday 23rd

You may be close to your inner compass today but can view it as an outsider and be more objective. You won't be fooled again. You may now be more aware of when someone is trying to trick you or dumb you down with excuses. Now is the time to stand up and be counted.

Thursday 24th

A new moon in your sign is a wonderful time to make goals and intentions regarding you and you alone. Your ruler, Jupiter, turns direct today too. This is an auspicious day and what you set in motion now will prosper and bring you joy. Mark this day on your calendar.

Friday 25th

You could feel the effects of your recent traumas today. All you need to do is relax. Don't try pushing forward or starting new schemes and projects. Let yourself simply 'be'. This may have taken a toll on your health, so take a day to unwind and recharge your batteries.

Saturday 26th

Your own home may be your refuge today. Sit quietly and look around you. You could be secretly plotting your next big project, but there's no rush to act on it today. Use your imagination and envisage what your home would look like if you had a clean slate to work with.

Sunday 27th

Let yourself dream about doing something new. You may be considering a new fitness regime or a healthier daily routine. If you're in the mood to switch something up, try it out first. Make small changes, move furniture around and freshen up your looks. Get creative.

Monday 28th

Conversations can be light and cheerful now. Networking with others can give you food for thought. Write them down and file them away for next year. Remember that you're in the planning stages and the more thought you give it, the better the results will be. Follow guidelines and good advice.

Tuesday 29th

If you've been seeking a teacher or guru. You may find them today. A person may appear who you respect greatly, and you may attach yourself to them as you know they have something to teach you. Your eyes and ears are open for anything new and adventurous.

Wednesday 30th

You're being asked to merge with the collective or your family now. The lone wolf approach may not work well today, so stick with your tribe and accept the love and care you receive there. Sometimes, you need to remember that you're the product of those who came before you.

DECEMBER

Thursday 1st

There may be some conflict or tension today. Your instinct is to put your own needs first and forget anyone who is disagreeable. However, it may be you who is being awkward. Check in with your inner compass and look at your actions objectively. You may just need to be more flexible.

Friday 2nd

Your thought processes could be hazy now as you cling to a dream that is no longer meant for you. Find it within yourself to move on with an open heart and a willingness to learn your place in the wider world. Get ready for some romance and a little bit of art this weekend.

Saturday 3rd

You have sufficient energy to make a good start on issues that have been on hold recently. Tread carefully in relationships and keep all communications clear and precise. Your desires are there for you to obtain, but remember to respect all boundaries, yours and others'.

Sunday 4th

Neptune, your inner compass, turns direct today and the fog will start to dissipate. You may need to have an inner dialogue with yourself and make sure you have an action plan. If you hesitate, it may be because you need to adjust, and this was something you might not have planned for.

Monday 5th

There may be something you need to do within your family circle now. This could be a group effort which has been neglected or skimmed over. Perhaps you didn't know how to progress, but you do now. You could be surprised by how easily the answer comes to you today.

Tuesday 6th

Speak to someone who can guide you up your personal mountain. You may have to deal with a financial issue such as an investment or a big purchase. If money needs to go out, make sure it's wisely spent. Large indulgences could set you back and trip you up.

Wednesday 7th

Enjoy a reasonably calm day, but reach out and make important connections. You could be in need of a financial advisor or someone who knows what they're doing regarding home renovations. Gather your research and make a vision board. Plot your ideas before implementing them. Get the broader picture together.

Thursday 8th

A full moon could highlight any issues in your relationship. You would be wise not to react to anything. Perhaps sleeping on it could give you a solution. You may have too many ideas floating around in your head. This is not the time to settle for one plan of action.

Friday 9th

You might struggle today and could have a crisis of conscience. This could make you want to retreat into your safety zone for a while. If you need time to process how you feel, switch off from your duties and plan to nurture yourself. Feed your soul and your mind will be at peace.

Saturday 10th

Today you can start building your empire. Venus has shifted into your values and finances area. You could get a better sense of what you desire and how to finance it. Good food and company are on the agenda today. Gather your closest allies for a movie and take-away.

Sunday 11th

You may have had too much of a good thing and wish to get back in control. Use the remainder of the weekend to do something you enjoy, but join the rest of the world outside your duvet. Your courage and high spirits may return by evening.

Monday 12th

Learn from elders or people in authority today. You could be connecting with someone who can give you the benefit of their experience. Your community can teach you a lot if you step outside and offer your services. You can show your leadership strengths and may find a role that suits you.

Tuesday 13th

It's important that you remember not to do everything by yourself now. Although you are capable of working alone, and often do, you need to fit in with the collective and take a minor role. This is a learning experience and will add skills to your resume.

Wednesday 14th

Your focus changes and you can be more practical and methodical now. If asked to be flexible, you may find this difficult. Stick with working with your hands or making solid, long-term plans. A challenge must be accepted, but as this is no quick fix, you must dedicate yourself to hard work.

Thursday 15th

Don't let your natural passion die down. People respect you for it. However, more earthy energy suggests that your way forward is by being grounded and focused. A new fitness regime can be what you need to fix yourself to a plan and see it through to the end.

Friday 16th

Although you're quite happy doing practical work, you may yearn to get away and do something more artistic. Plan for time with your friendship groups this weekend and kick off the festive season with some fun and laughter. You could simply need to let off some steam with your social tribe.

Saturday 17th

Work may be on your mind, but you should use this weekend to unwind. If money matters concern you, rein in your spending and keep it simple. A discussion with someone who may be a professional could help to put a few things straight. Think outside the box and accept any suggestions offered.

Sunday 18th

You may resort to a trusted friend to help you think through your strategies. Phone calls and visits to people you haven't seen for some time can bear fruit. Be sociable but also pick other's brains for ideas you can build on in the future. Share your ideas with them too.

Monday 19th

You may need some quiet time as your cogs could be turning. Picking apart new concepts and rebuilding them for yourself could fill your mind now. Remember to put things down on paper or they could be lost as your mind never fixes on one idea for very long.

Tuesday 20th

Think about what skills you've acquired in the past which could be resurrected now. You may find that something or someone from the past comes in use. Deep thinking can produce something unexpected, but which aligns with your core values. Keep it going if it suits your needs.

Wednesday 21st

The winter solstice arrives today and gives you a chance to pause and reflect on the year gone by. As the Sun enters your area concerning property and values, it would be a good time to seriously think about what you need to do to enhance your life.

Thursday 22nd

Put your personal dreams to one side today and consider your duties to others. There may have been unnecessary tension with a partnership recently, but you can remedy this by planning for quality time together over the festive season. Do something which you both love and a shared dream might present itself.

Friday 23rd

The new moon is your opportunity to set intentions around building up your empire and making it as solid as you can. Bring together your practical skills and ability to see a project through to the end. There's no need to set anything in motion just yet.

Saturday 24th

This is a lovely day where the planetary energy suggests that home is where the heart is. You could be extra busy today. Perhaps you're hosting the celebrations and making sure that your home is welcoming. You can showcase your skills and authority now. Add your own unique touch to the day.

Sunday 25th

Today you may be more connected to your community than you realise. Although you may be frazzled and have some anxiety, you can stay in control by inviting your tribe to contribute in their own ways. Your ruler, Jupiter, blesses you with joy, optimism and abundance. Just don't overdo the good things.

Monday 26th

You might experience some inner tension now, but this could simply be tiredness. You might want to leave any chores for the day and come back to them when the party is over. Your sense of responsibility to others is high and they will respect you for it.

Tuesday 27th

As the Moon moves into your family zone you may think you've had enough and need to do your own thing today. However, you can comply with requests for your company and all will work out well. Nobody expects anything from you. You are surrounded by unconditional love.

Wednesday 28th

Expect a late surprise or two today as your responsibilities and personal goals merge. By evening you should feel perfectly in line with your inner compass and can rest easy knowing you've done your best and those around you are satisfied. Reward yourself with something you love doing or a personal treat.

Thursday 29th

Mercury turns retrograde before the year ends. Remember not to commit to anything if it isn't to your liking. Try not to push your own agenda as you could clash with someone important and cause unnecessary stress. You could be a little selfish today.

Friday 30th

Take another day of rest and put all your plans on hold. You may not have the energy to do anything much and will be annoyed if you don't finish something you started. Go slowly with a partner as they could be feeling this too. Enjoy what's left of the holidays.

Saturday 31st

The energy isn't favourable today. If you don't want to party, you don't have to. You could feel that someone is being demanding and will need to put your foot down firmly. End the year doing what you want to do and not what another has dictated for you.

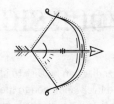

Sagittarius

· · · · · · · · · · · · · ·

PEOPLE WHO SHARE
YOUR SIGN

PEOPLE WHO SHARE YOUR SIGN

The free spirits of the zodiac can be easy to identify with their expansive thinking and lively approach to life. From Winston Churchill to Nicki Minaj, it feels like these inspiring Sagittarians where placed on Earth to motivate the masses. Whether this dual sign is influenced more by their intellectual mind or their physical strength, Sagittarians' daring attitudes will see them go far. Discover which of these optimistic Sagittarians share your exact birthday and see if you can spot the similarities.

November 23rd
Alexis Ren (1996), Miley Cyrus (1992), Snooki (1987), Kelly Brook (1979), Zoë Ball (1970), Vincent Cassel (1966), Nicolás Maduro, Venezuelan President (1962), John Schnatter (1961), Ludovico Einaudi (1955)

November 24th
Sarah Hyland (1990), Katherine Heigl (1978), Colin Hanks (1977), Stephen Merchant (1974), Shirley Henderson (1965), Billy Connolly (1942), Dale Carnegie (1888), Henri de Toulouse-Lautrec (1864)

November 25th
Katie Cassidy (1986), Gaspard Ulliel (1984), Joel Kinnaman (1979), Christina Applegate (1971), John F. Kennedy Jr. (1960), Ben Stein (1944), Ricardo Montalbán (1920), Karl Benz (1844)

November 26th

Rita Ora (1990), Danny Welbeck (1990), Tamsin Egerton (1988), Chris Hughes (1983), DJ Khaled (1975), Peter Facinelli (1973), Tina Turner (1939), Charles M. Schulz (1922)

November 27th

Professor Green (1983), Robin Givens (1964), Yulia Tymoshenko, Ukrainian Prime Minister (1960), William Fichtner (1956), Jil Sander (1943), Manolo Blahnik (1942), Jimi Hendrix (1942), Bruce Lee (1940)

November 28th

Karen Gillan (1987), Trey Songz (1984), Mary Elizabeth Winstead (1984), Daniel Henney (1979), Jon Stewart (1962), Martin Clunes (1961), Alfonso Cuarón (1961), Judd Nelson (1959), Ed Harris (1950), Friedrich Engels (1820)

November 29th

Diego Boneta (1990), Lauren German (1978), Chadwick Boseman (1977), Anna Faris (1976), Ryan Giggs (1973), Don Cheadle (1964), Jacques Chirac, French President (1932), Jackie Stallone (1921), C. S. Lewis (1898)

November 30th

Kaley Cuoco (1985), Chrissy Teigen (1985), Elisha Cuthbert (1982), Steve Aoki (1977), Ben Stiller (1965), Gary Lineker (1960), Billy Idol (1955), Ridley Scott (1937), Winston Churchill (1874), Lucy Maud Montgomery (1874), Mark Twain (1835)

December 1st

Chanel Iman (1990), Zoë Kravitz (1988), Vance Joy (1987), Janelle Monáe (1985), Sarah Silverman (1970), Pablo Escobar (1949), Bette Midler (1945), Woody Allen (1935)

December 2nd

Charlie Puth (1991), Alfred Enoch (1988), Teairra Marí (1987), Action Bronson (1983), Aaron Rodgers (1983), Britney Spears (1981), Nelly Furtado (1978), Lucy Liu (1968)

December 3rd

Amanda Seyfried (1985), Dascha Polanco (1982), Jenna Dewan (1980), Holly Marie Combs (1973), Brendan Fraser (1968), Daryl Hannah (1960), Julianne Moore (1960), Ozzy Osbourne (1948)

December 4th

Niykee Heaton (1994), Tyra Banks (1973), Kevin Sussman (1970), Jay-Z (1969), Fred Armisen (1966), Marisa Tomei (1964), Jeff Bridges (1949), Albert Bandura (1925)

December 5th

Anthony Martial (1995), Frankie Muniz (1985), Ronnie O'Sullivan (1975), Paula Patton (1975), Eddie the Eagle (1963), King Bhumibol the Great of Thailand (1927), Walt Disney (1901), Werner Heisenberg (1901)

December 6th

Stefanie Scott (1996), Alberto Contador (1982), Noel Clarke (1975), Sarah Rafferty (1972), Judd Apatow (1967), Nick Park (1958), Peter Buck (1956), Agnes Moorehead (1900)

December 7th

Nicholas Hoult (1989), Emily Browning (1988), Aaron Carter (1987), Dan Bilzerian (1980), John Terry (1980), Sara Bareilles (1979), Jennifer Carpenter (1979), Noam Chomsky (1928)

December 8th

AnnaSophia Robb (1993), Amir Khan (1986), Nicki Minaj (1982), Ian Somerhalder (1978), Dominic Monaghan (1976), Sinéad O'Connor (1966), Teri Hatcher (1964), Kim Basinger (1953), John Banville (1945)

December 9th

Simon Helberg (1980), Jesse Metcalfe (1978), Kurt Angle (1968), Felicity Huffman (1962), Donny Osmond (1957), John Malkovich (1953), Dame Judi Dench (1934), Kirk Douglas (1916)

December 10th

Teyana Taylor (1990), Gonzalo Higuaín (1987), Kim Sears (1987), Raven-Symoné (1985), Emmanuelle Chriqui (1975), Susanna Reid (1970), Kenneth Branagh (1960), Michael Clarke Duncan (1957), Emily Dickinson (1830)

December 11th

Hailee Steinfeld (1996), Mos Def (1973), Mo'Nique (1967), DJ Yella (1967), Marco Pierre White (1961), Nikki Sixx (1958), Jermaine Jackson (1954), Pranab Mukherjee, Indian President (1935)

December 12th

Yuvraj Singh (1981), Mayim Bialik (1975), Mädchen Amick (1970), Jennifer Connelly (1970), Regina Hall (1970), Sheila E. (1957), Bill Nighy (1949), Frank Sinatra (1915), Edvard Munch (1863)

December 13th

Katherine Schwarzenegger (1989), Taylor Swift (1989), Amy Lee (1981), Tom DeLonge (1975), Jamie Foxx (1967), Steve Buscemi (1957), Christopher Plummer (1929), Dick Van Dyke (1925)

December 14th

Tori Kelly (1992), Vanessa Hudgens (1988), Michael Owen (1979), Miranda Hart (1972), Natascha McElhone (1969), Dilma Rousseff, Brazilian President (1947), Jane Birkin (1946), Stan Smith (1946), B. K. S. Iyengar (1918), King George VI of the United Kingdom (1895)

December 15th

Jesse Lingard (1992), Keylor Navas (1986), Camilla Luddington (1983), Charlie Cox (1982), Michelle Dockery (1981), Adam Brody (1979), Don Johnson (1949), Tim Conway (1933), Gustave Eiffel (1832)

December 16th

Zara Larsson (1997), Anna Popplewell (1988), Theo James (1984), Danielle Lloyd (1983), Krysten Ritter (1981), Miranda Otto (1967), Benjamin Bratt (1963), Philip K. Dick (1928), Wassily Kandinsky (1866)

December 17th

Dynamo (1982), Katheryn Winnick (1977), Milla Jovovich (1975), Sarah Paulson (1974), Giovanni Ribisi (1974), Rian Johnson (1973), Eugene Levy (1946), Muhammadu Buhari, Nigerian President (1942), Pope Francis (1936)

December 18th

Ashley Benson (1989), Christina Aguilera (1980), Katie Holmes (1978), Sia Furler (1975), DMX (1970), Brad Pitt (1963), Jonathan Cainer (1957), Ray Liotta (1954), Steven Spielberg (1946), Keith Richards (1943), J. J. Thomson (1856)

December 19th

Alexis Sánchez (1988), Karim Benzema (1987), Jake Gyllenhaal (1980), Alyssa Milano (1972), Tyson Beckford (1970), Richard Hammond (1969), Jennifer Beals (1963), Til Schweiger (1963), Maurice White (1941), Édith Piaf (1915)

December 20th

JoJo (1990), Bugzy Malone (1990), Bob Morley (1984), Jonah Hill (1983), Lara Stone (1983), Ashley Cole (1980), Chris Robinson (1966), Jenny Agutter (1952), Uri Geller (1946), Peter Criss (1945)

December 21st

Steven Yeun (1983), Tom Payne (1982), Emmanuel Macron, French President (1977), Kiefer Sutherland (1966), Ray Romano (1957), Jane Kaczmarek (1955), Chris Evert (1954), Samuel L. Jackson (1948), Jane Fonda (1937), Phil Donahue (1935)